Radical Islam Why?

Confronting Jihad at Home & Abroad

Dr. Jeffrey F. Addicott
Lt. Colonel (U.S. Army, ret.)
B.A., J.D., LL.M., S.J.D.

Lawyers & Judges
Publishing Company, Inc.
Tucson, Arizona

 Lawyers & Judges
Publishing Company, Inc.
P.O. Box 30040 • Tucson, AZ 85751-0040
(800) 209-7109 • FAX (800) 330-8795
e-mail: sales@lawyersandjudges.com
www.lawyersandjudges.com

Library of Congress Cataloging-in-Publication Data

Addicott, Jeffrey F., author.
Radical Islam -- why? : confronting jihad at home & abroad / Jeffrey F. Addicott.
   pages cm
Includes index.
ISBN 978-1-936360-56-7 (softcover : alk. paper) -- ISBN 1-936360-56-X (softcover : alk. paper)
1. Terrorism--Religious aspects--Islam. 2. Islamic fundamentalism. 3. Jihad. I. Title.
BP190.5.T47A33 2016
363.325--dc23
                              2015036066

ISBN 13: 978-1-936360-56-7
ISBN 10: 1-936360-56-X

Printed in the United States of America
10 9 8 7 6 5 4 3

Dedication

R.B. Thieme, Jr. (1918-2009) —

pivot of the nation, theologian, soldier, educator,

patriot

Contents

Acknowledgments

Among the colleagues and friends who have supported this book with their insight, time, and thoughtfulness are Teresa B. Addicott and Colonel G. Michael Stripling. The author also wishes to acknowledge the invaluable support of my sister, Deborah E. Addicott, who provided a generous financial gift which funded the construction of a state-of-the-art research facility which houses the Center for Terrorism Law.

Among the colleagues, students and friends who expertly dealt with editing and conceptual, bibliographical, and organizational problems are Brittney Baldovinos, Brittanny Perrigue, Landon Keating, Paul Cooper, and Ramon Macias.

Title page artwork by Aiden F. Dunbar.

Preface

"The trouble with man is twofold, he cannot learn those truths that are too complicated, and he forgets those truths that are too simple."[1]

— Rebecca West

Americans of age recall exactly where they were on that morning of September 11, 2001. That was the day 19 members of the radical Islamic group al-Qa'eda attacked America from the skies and incinerated 3,000 people. As a new law professor at St. Mary's University School of Law, in San Antonio, Texas, I was working on my second cup of coffee with the love of my life, my very pregnant wife. The television was turned on in the living room but both of us were focused on getting me get out the door to teach my morning class on Federal Civil Procedure (our one year old son was somehow still asleep).

Then we saw it; like a promo for a bad action movie, the news channel was reporting that a plane had crashed into one of the Twin Towers in New York City. As a former Army staff officer who was deeply involved in terrorism issues during my twenty years of service, my gut feeling told me that it was not an accident, but a terror attack. When we saw in real time a second aircraft plow into the other tower, I knew the culprits — radical Islam.

Indeed, not only had I served a quarter of my career in the Army as the senior legal advisor to the U.S. Army Special Forces (Green Berets) dealing with the legal and tactical aspects of terrorism, in 2000 I had published a chapter in a book for the US Army War

1. Rebecca West (Cicely Isabel Fairfield), THE MEANING OF TREASON 311 (1949).

College detailing the group al-Qa'eda and the imminent threat they posed to the United States homeland by means of a massive terror attack.[2]

At first, some Americans were deeply incredulous about the cause of the attack. When it became clear that the terrorists were members of the Afghan-based group called al-Qa'eda the nation quickly closed ranks and supported President George W. Bush's plan to counter strike them with a heavy military blow. But as we soon discovered, it was more than just bombing a rogue Islamist terrorist group "over there;" the United States was quickly faced with a plethora of legal and policy issues associated with how to deal with a much bigger threat. What President Bush euphemistically dubbed the "War on Terror," was on.

After 15 years and two major combat missions in the Middle East costing over 50,000 Americans in dead and wounded, the War on Terror is still with us today. Amazingly, while everyone is cognizant of the term War on Terror, almost no one understands what it really means. What is this War on Terror? Is it a war against the tactic of terrorism? Is it a war against all terror groups? Is it a war against Islamic terror groups only? Is it a war against Islam itself? Furthermore, even the use of the word "war" has raised its own set of questions. Is the word employed as a simplistic metaphor, like the war on drugs or the war on poverty, or does the word war really mean that this is a real war to be fought under the law of war? And if so ... who is the enemy? Who *is* the enemy?

In his book the *Art of War*, the great military genius Sun Tzu emphatically warned that battles cannot consistently be won unless you know your enemy.[3] He was spot on.

The purpose of this book is to fully explore the nature of the enemy forces arrayed against us so that we can find better ways to confront them. In its broadest sense, the enemy is best encapsulated by the simple term *radical Islam*, with the *jihadist* serving as

2. *Terrorism and Weapons of Mass Destruction: A Review and New Paradigm*, in Transnational Threats: Blending Law Enforcement and Military Strategies, 105 (Carolyn W. Pumphrey, Ed., 2000).
3. Sun-tzu, Art of War (Ralph D. Sawuer, Trans., 1994).

their foot-soldier of death. Whether the jihadist follows al-Qa'eda,
ISIS, al-Shabaab, Boko Haram, Hamas, Islamic Jihad, Abu Sayyaf,
Ansaru, Jemaah Islamiyah, Hezbollah, Al-Nusra, Muslim Brotherhood, Ahle Sunnat Wal Jamaat, the Iranian mullahs, or any of the
other scores and scores of Islamist terror organizations, the enemy
is radical Islam. They are all poisonous branches of the same poison tree.

As we shall explore, each individual Islamist group requires tai-
lored short-term strategies to blunt them, but all of our antagonists
are infected with the same religious virus of radical Islam. Some,
like al-Qa'eda and Taliban, qualify to be treated as unlawful enemy
combatants[4] while others do not and operate independently. Some
spring from the majority *Sunni* brand of Islam and some from the
Shia brand. All fight zealously for the revival of the Muslim caliphate and the supremacy of Islam and its draconian code—*Sharia
Law*. They believe that this is the will of their god *Allah*.

The task of exploring and discussing radical Islam seems easy
enough to formulate and present for rational debate, but it is not.
In our current culture where many like free speech but don't like to
stand for it, there exists great reluctance to intellectually address the
who, what, where, when, how, and why of radical Islam. Too many
in America today either live and speak in terms of expediency or
are in denial.

While a few may be honest enough to acknowledge the hard
fact that radical Islam is the number one terror threat to the United States, they absolutely refuse to speak openly about the core
base-line religious beliefs of radical Islam that both condones and
commands murder and genocide in the name of religion. This phenomenon of silence is more than a reluctance of running afoul of
the time honored manners of social interaction—the old saw that
religion and politics must never be mentioned in polite conversation. (To be sure, most people of faith do not like their religious
beliefs scrutinized and extend that courtesy to other belief systems
as well.) The deafening silence when it comes to radical Islam is

4. *See* Jeffrey F Addicott, TERRORISM LAW: MATERIALS, CASES, COMMENTS, 61-
191 (7th ed. 2014).

also the by-product of what the use of terror tactics is all about—the goal of the terrorist is to kill one and frighten ten thousand. People are simply too afraid to speak out about the religious bedrock that supports radical Islam.

Then there is the factor of incredulity. The avowed aim of conquering the world for Allah is disregarded not only because of its sheer improbability, but Western nations simply refuse to actualize the notion that in the modern "enlightened" age anyone would actually wage war based purely on a religious belief. Subjugating other people, beheadings, suicide bombings, sex slavery of mothers and their daughters, mass murder of innocent husbands and their sons, this is stuff straight out of the Dark Ages!

In addition, the secular multicultural world completely marginalizes the notion of killing others in order to gain the approbation of God because in their view all religions are deemed to be benign. To their way of thinking, religious people achieve heaven by performing a system of human good deeds with a few rituals and taboos thrown in for good measure, not violence.[5] Even many Muslims cannot come to grips with the reality of a radical and violent Islam that is deeply seated in authentic Islamic theology. For example, just after the January 2015 murders in Paris by radical Islamists, one of America's self-described "celebrity Muslims," Kareem Abdul-Jabbar, wrote a commentary piece for *Time* naively entitled, "Paris Was Not About Religion."

> For me, religion – no matter which one – is ultimately about people wanting to live humble, moral lives that create a harmonious community and promote tolerance and friendship. All religious rules should be in service of this goal. The Islam I learned and practice does just that.[6]

---

5. *See* Thomas S. Kidd, *Who Is, Or Isn't Going to Hell?*, USA TODAY, May 23, 2011, at A11 (discussing the idea that some Christians believe God will allow all humans entry into heaven regardless of their beliefs or deeds).
6. Kareem Abdul-Jabbar, *Paris Was Not About Religion*, TIME, January 26, 2015, at 29.

Of course, overriding all the multifarious factors promoting silence of discussion about radical Islam is the insidiousness of "political correctness."[7] Before that secular Deity, progressives smugly demand that we fall to our knees and tremble. Under the doctrine of political correctness, it is *verboten* to engage in any form of dialogue that is even remotely critical of Islam. Critiques of Christianity or Judaism are allowed in the market place of free speech but never Islam.

Consequences of disagreeing with this orthodoxy of silence about any aspect of the religion of Islam are severe. Those that do exhibit the temerity to point out the fact that certain written tenants of Islam's *Koran* clearly spell out unequivocal commands for the murder of innocent civilians will find themselves branded by *ad hominem* attacks as Islamophobics, bigots, racists, fear-mongers, etc.

Strangely, those who actually commit horrendous hate crimes in the name of Allah are never subjected to any "name calling." At most they are just the "terrorists."

Numerous well-funded religious and secular advocacy groups in the United States make it their business to track, intimidate, ridicule, and silence any who cast Islam in a negative light. Just as a jungle canopy occludes the light of day, these committed ideologues serve to darken free thinking and free speech. It does not speak well of our society that such advocacy groups who proclaim to be against "intolerance" of all brands and so very tolerant of radical Islam. They won't even call the jihadi violence a "hate" crime, that term is especially reserved for only right-wing extremist terrorism.

Accordingly, in the face of the hot fires of political correctness many in our society—to include our highest leadership figures—simply censor themselves when it comes to radical Islam. They will say nothing about radical Islam beyond parroting the worn out

---

7. Janet Hook, *Carson Defends Opposition to Muslim President*, WALL STREET JOURNAL, September 23, 2015, at A4 (Ben Carson argues that political correctness was to blame for his view that certain Islamic tenets are inconsistent with the U.S. Constitution after the Council on American-Islamic Relations demanded he "quit the presidential race").

phrase: "Islam is a religion of peace." In the kindest sense, they stealthily self-censor in the name of accommodation, civility, or tolerance. Considering the clear and present threat posed by radical Islam in our age of weapons of mass destruction, this expediency is either abject cowardice or sincere self-deception.

Anticipating the opprobrium that this book is sure to generate, I think it appropriate to encapsulate at the inception what I do and do not advocate. Although I am well-schooled in military science, I am now a legal educator by profession. As such, I approach this matter armed with well over 30 years of experience in dealing with terrorist groups both in the real world of combat operations and in the arena of public discourse.

First, I am convinced that the evidence is conclusive and incontrovertible. Radical Islam is and will continue to be the number one terror threat to the United States for many years hence.

Second, radical Islam must be fought with all available resources. In order to do this it is imperative that the underlying theology is laid out on the table and thoroughly understood. Those who are unwilling to expend the intellectual effort to address radical Islam will invariably argue that such an endeavor is at best a monumental waste of time, i.e., it can't be done, or at worst a mean-spirited journey into divisiveness. The divisiveness complaint can be brushed aside without much comment—truth is intrinsic in nature and will always create spectacular divisions. Truth is seldom a unifier.

Likewise, the argument that the task is just too difficult holds little merit. One need not be a Muslim scholar to understand radical Islam, the application of critical thinking skills will suffice. Contrary to what might be imagined, access to the theological orthodoxy of radical Islam is readily available to the general public and does not rely on tortured interpretations of Islamic writings and teachings. In fact, the layman needs to do very little in terms of gathering the baseline religious information because the proponents of radical Islam will tell you exactly where to find it. Islamists saturate their rhetoric with theological passages that quote the specific texts and traditions formulated and commanded through their leader and founder Muhammad.

Mainstream Muslims like Kareem Abdul-Jabbar can reject the tenants of radical Islam; nearly all do. But they cannot pretend that it isn't based on specific parameters found in Islam. Coupled with the historical examples set by Muhammad himself, jihadists self-identify with clear bright line theological precepts woven throughout Muslim text and tradition.

Jihadists are what scholars in the legal profession would label as "strict constructionists." They interpret the text from the seventh century perspective of the original intent of the writer. Period. For them the religious passages do not evolve or change over time with new interpretations to fit new environments. Thus, *Radical Islam Why?* will provide an outline overview of the strict constructionist theology of Islam that provides the justification for radical Islam.

Although information is drawn from a wide variety of sources, every effort has been made to make the materials concise and as readable as possible. In addition, not each and every argument related to pertinent historical, legal, or theological disciplines are detailed. While my critics will undoubtedly complain that I am "not giving the other side" equal weight, my answer to such is quite simple. I don't give the "other side" much script because most Americans live in the other side each and every day of their lives. The zealots of political correctness put it in the water. The information presented in these pages is seldom expressed. Again, a central goal of the book is to give a "CAT scan" to the core concepts of radical Islam in a manner that is seldom expressed.

Third, I believe that there is a significant difference between radical Islam and Islam. As a 2009 *Time* magazine article noted, "the veil is not the suicide vest."[8] I agree, but would amend that statement to read "the veil is not *necessarily* the suicide vest." Without question, although many Muslims around the world willingly accept a strict conservative version of Islam, to include the full weight of Sharia Law, this does not mean that they will commit murder and terror to spread those beliefs. On the other hand, those Muslims that do employ violence to spread Islam are therefore properly labeled

---

8.   Fareed Zakaria, *Learning to Live with Radical Islam*, NEWSWEEK, March 9, 2009, at 28.

with the term *radical Islam*. Thus, all conservative Muslims are not radical Muslims, but all radical Muslims are certainly ultra-conservative Muslims.

In this context, Muslims should not be faulted for a desire to spread their religion to all mankind, called *Da'wa*. Indeed, as a Christian I would certainly wish to see all humans believe in Christ for salvation. The gravamen of the matter is how one goes about spreading that religious belief to others. By peaceful dialogue or by the sword?

At the end of the day, the issue is not whether the Muslim religion is intrinsically violent in its religious dictates, even though many numbers of them absolutely believe that it is; rather, the concern is what the billion plus Muslims around the world believe and how many of them are willing to provide actual or material support to terrorism. How widespread is the problem?

Fourth, as the title suggests, solutions will also be proffered. Obviously, an effective strategy to confront radical Islam must begin with knowing who they are. To be paralyzed in our thinking, as we have been for so long now, is disastrous. Without a lucid understanding of the theology of radical Islam, the United States cannot hope to realistically confront jihadists either here in the homeland or abroad. Only then can the civilized community mount a spirited defense that is both active and passive, to address the short and long term solutions to radical Islam. As a military axiom, you cannot defeat the enemy until you do two things: (1) identify the enemy, and (2) identify the enemy's center of gravity.

I also argue that the most formidable counterstroke to diffuse the religion of radical Islam is the grace-religion of Christianity. Apart from addressing the ultimate question of life under the rubric of grace (the eternal salvation of the human soul), its collateral temporal message of tolerance and freedom of religion provides a brilliant antidote for rebuffing the vicious intolerance of radical Islam. In freedom-based nations like the United States, freedom of religion is a sacred concept that the framers of the Constitution took straight from the pages of the Bible's New Testament.[9] Americans

9. *See generally* AMERICA'S GOD AND COUNTRY ENCYCLOPEDIA OF QUOTATIONS (1994).

are free to worship any god, or, no god, without fear of persecution from the State or from fellow citizens. Most Muslim-majority nations cannot make such a boast.

Finally, radical Islam cannot be ignored or wished away; it is a fact of the times in which we live. It is the evil of our time. How we face radical Islam will determine much about our own national future and the future of millions of our fellow humans around the world. Tragically, too many Americans have succumbed to the foolishness of magical thinking in their assessment of radical Islam as a minor fanatical, non-religious movement with few adherents. For example, President Obama has referred to ISIS, a vicious radical Islamic group, variously, as a "jay-vee team" or "not Islamic," statements that are disoriented to reality and a disservice to the truth, however well intentioned.

At its heart radical Islam is a religious belief that not only vehemently opposes our way of life in the West, and seeks to murder us wholesale if it can, but opposes any deviation from what it calls the "true Islam." In the purity of their belief system, they have killed more Muslims (apostates) than Christians or Jews (infidels).

It is time for transparency of thinking and firmness of action. It is time to look radical Islam straight in the eye. We can no longer sacrifice objective thought on the altar of "agenda driven" political correctness. If we do, the horrors of 9/11 were only the opening salvo in the War on Terror.[10]

---

10. Kevin Johnson, *9/11 Panel: Terrorism Fight is in 'New and Dangerous Phase'*, USA TODAY, July 22, 2014, at A1 (marking the tenth anniversary of the 9/11 Commission Report, the 9/11 Commission reconvened and issued a warning that the "War on Terror" was entering a more dangerous phase due to the increased number of Islamic fighters from the Middle East and self-radicalized jihadists here in the United States).

Foreword

In this most professional and poignant endeavor Colonel Jeffrey Addicott uses his real world military and legal skills as a canvas on which to paint a concise, bold, and lucid discussion about the machinations of radical Islam. Those familiar with Professor Addicott know that he pulls no punches and this book will not disappoint. Given the emerging threat of weapons of mass destruction in the hands of terrorists, *Radical Islam Why?* is a cutting-edge book for our day. Professor Addicott has done us all—educators, the military, and the wider public—a great service in detailing the necessity to apply key historical lessons in our strategy to address the rising tide of radical Islam.

— Major General Alfred A. Valenzuela (US Army, ret.)

Chapter 1

Lexicon of Terror and Terrorism

"The goal of the terrorist is to kill one and frighten 10,000."
—Chinese proverb

Out of the world's opposing ideas that seek to explain the nature and function of man on planet earth, I chose early on to adopt the conservative view. Liberals think in terms of subjectivity and place great weight in the notion that the "environment" is the root cause of man's problems and that moral issues in life are relative in nature. At their heart, liberals are utopians and in America this idea can be traced to the Pilgrims ever striving to create a better world, believing that the "evil" in man and society can be overcome and that a perfect people and country can be achieved by reform(s).

Conservatives don't adhere to utopianism because, quite plainly, they don't believe in it. Understanding that individuals are born flawed, not made flawed, they believe in the efficacy of absolute moral templates to direct their lives in a flawed world. In America, the chief road map for navigating the world is the Bible.[1] As quoted in the Preface of the book, the English author Rebecca West knew that life's governing truths were objective and simple. West also

---

1. For an excellent discussion see H. W. Crocker III, ROBERT E. LEE ON LEADERSHIP 14–15(1999).

realized that the never ending problem rests not in the principles of conservatism but rather with flawed people adhering to them.

Clear thinkers understand that societal rules of conduct are made for the general principle, not for the exception. For example, the fact that an innocent person is killed in a gun accident or a crime does not mean that guns should be outlawed or unduly restricted by the State. The general principle, as enshrined in the Second Amendment to the Constitution, holds that the right to bear firearms is an absolute necessity to guarantee individual and national freedom under a consent form of government.

Furthermore, I was fortunate to have been exposed to the benefits that accrue from growing up in a military family (my father was a Navy officer for 30 years) and later serving for 20 years in the Army myself. One of the refreshing things about the military lifestyle is that it tends to orient one to the base realities of life and lends credibility to those explanations that hit the bottom line as rapidly and as simply as possible. Soldiers generally can spot a phony—person or argument—rather quickly.

Thus, when it comes to pedagogy, I am a firm believer in the validity of "don't hide the ball," even though as a legal scholar I certainly have my "law professor" language that can wax eloquent with twenty-dollar words and run-on prepositional phrases that swirl like dust devils on a west Texas landscape. Some may not understand what I am saying, but it sure sounds educated!

When I am truly engaged in imparting thought, I prefer my "military language." It communicates. For example, the junior line officer that instructs his troops with fancy rhetoric to "ambulate up the hill with all alacrity," will get blank looks. Better results flow when the lieutenant yells to his men: "Get your sorry ____ up the damn hill now!" Properly using the proper vocabulary is essential.

Syntax is the study of words with the vocabulary of language a necessary component of intellect. The human body is real and material; the human soul is real but immaterial. While the soul possesses self-awareness, conscience, emotion, volition, and intelligence, the thinking capabilities associated with the brain requires vocabulary in order to function efficiently. Accordingly, before anything can be intelligently discussed it must be identified and defined as to its meaning. Unfortunately, much of the subject of terror and terrorism is plagued by lack of clear definition. To be certain, the term terrorism carries with it tremendous definitional baggage.

Meanwhile, Back at the United Nations

If you remember nothing else about terrorism, know that it is a *tactic*.[2] Despite the many descriptive uses of the term terrorism, it is and always will be a tactic. It is an action carried out by a person(s).

Although many trace the etymology of the word terror to France's "reign of terror" under Robespierre and the Jacobin Committee of Public Safety (*regime de la terreur*), the employment of the tactic of terror is a phenomenon that has been around for a very long time in human history. Notwithstanding the fact that terrorism is the antithesis of the rule of law, there exists no consensus on a precise definition of terrorism either in the international community or in the United States. This is due in part to the tensions of the Cold War era when West and East could agree on precious little, but also continues today under the postmodernist cliché, "one man's terrorist is another man's freedom fighter." For instance, a Palestinian suicide bomber in Israel who intentionally kills innocent Jewish civilians may simultaneously be considered a "hero" by certain segments of the Palestinian population and a murderer by others.

The concept of terrorism is now firmly embedded in the daily lexicon. Yet there is still no accepted international definition. Reflecting the politics associated with reaching a global definition for terrorism, the international community's United Nations has failed miserably. The track record of the United Nations shows that it prefers to avoid the term terrorism altogether, use it in a general sense only, or to carefully carve out very specific acts in selected international treaties to characterize as "terrorism." The issue of using violence against civilians in so-called wars of "national liberation"

---

2. *See* Caleb Carr, THE LESSONS OF TERROR: A HISTORY OF WARFARE AGAINST CIVILIANS 17–30 (2002) (discussing how terrorism is a tactic associated with violence in war and peace).

remains a perennial stumbling block. In turn, definitional agreement seems always hindered by whether or not terrorist events are viewed as working for or against one's own national, political, or religious interests.

In the wake of 9/11 two significant efforts were made by the international community to define the concept of terror and terrorism.[3] First, the United Nation's Ad Hoc Committee on Terrorism proposed a definition of terror for the General Assembly to adopt. The General Assembly was unable to reach majority consensus due in large part to strong opposition from the 56-member Organization of Islamic Cooperation (all Muslim nations) who insisted that any international definition of terrorism contain a fixed caveat.[4] The Organization of Islamic Cooperation demanded that the proposed international definition exempt all so-called wars of national liberation against foreign occupation, i.e., if the violence utilized is to further a "just cause," such as the ambiguous concept of national liberation, then acts of terror may be tolerated as legitimate expressions of resistance. This is patently absurd. Those familiar with the Organization of Islamic Cooperation already know its reputation for hypocrisy when it comes to terrorism; they define terrorism internally to exclude Israelis as victims of terrorism and exclude the terror groups of Hamas and Hezbollah as terrorists organizations.[5]

In failing to establish consensus in defining terrorism, the United Nations fell prey to the liberal's view of life in terms of relativity: that the end justifies the means. In other words, the slaughter of innocent civilians is justified because the cause is deemed to be just.[6]

---

3. U.N. Secretary-General, *In Larger Freedom: Towards Development, Security and Human Rights for All: Rep. of the Secretary-General*, ¶ 74–126, U.N. Doc. A/59/2005 (Mar. 21, 2005) (emphasizing why the United Nations needs to address and define terrorism as a collective body).
4. Colum Lynch, *Islamic Group Blocks Terror Treaty; Nations Demand U.N. Pact Exemption for Anti-Israeli Militants*, WASHINGTON POST, November 10, 2001, at A19.
5. Deborah Weiss, Commentary, *Obama Excludes Israel from Counterterrorism Group: Throwing an Ally Under the Bus*, WASHINGTON TIMES, September 21, 2012, at B.
6. Joshua Muravchik, Editorial, *The U.N.'s Terrorism Gap*, LOS ANGELES

While understanding the motivation and goal for the act is obviously important, motivation and goal should always be totally irrelevant in terms of justification. For instance, during the 1980s acts of public bombings and the murder of civilians (by burning the victims in tires) by the "Spear of the Nation," the armed wing of the African National Congress (ANC), were acts of terrorism. The ends — getting rid of apartheid — can never justify the means.

At least the Secretary General of the United Nations, Kofi Annan, correctly understood that the "cause" is not a factor in defining terrorism. Never adopted by the United Nations General Assembly, Annan proposed this wonderfully succinct definition in 2005:

> [A]ny action constitutes terrorism if it is intended to cause death or serious bodily harm to civilians or non-combatants, with the purpose of intimidating a population or compelling a Government or an international organization to do or abstain from doing any act.[7]

Second, on September 28, 2001, the United Nations Security Council adopted Resolution 1373. The resolution's requirements were meant to create a common legal basis for all States to take effective action against terrorists by criminalizing terrorist fundraising and blocking terrorist assets. Quite impressive on paper, Resolution 1373 requires all member States to "[r]efrain from providing any form of support, active or passive, to entities or persons involved in terrorist acts;" "take the necessary steps to prevent the commission of terrorist acts;" "deny safe haven to those who finance, plan, support, or commit terrorist acts;" and "prevent those who finance, plan, facilitate, or commit terrorist acts from using their respective territories for those purposes against other States or their citizens ...." To implement these obligations, a Counter-Terrorism Committee (CTC) consisting of 15-member States was

---

TIMES, September 18, 2005, at A5 (discussing Annan's proposed definition of terrorism and the Muslim States' rebuttal).

7. Estanislao Oziewicz, *Annan Proposes Definition of Terrorism*, CIGI (March 21, 2005), http://www.cigionline.org/articles/2005/03/annan-proposes-definition-terrorism.

created to receive hundreds of State reports on progress in each of the mentioned areas. Amazingly, 15 years later, the CTC has yet to name a single terrorist organization, individual, or State sponsor of terrorism, not one.

Common Sense Definition

If a universal definition is not possible, there is still the common sense practical definition. Since the victims of terrorism are invariably innocent civilians, it appears fundamentally logical that a definitional approach should concentrate on the act, with the political, religious, or social causes that motivate the act as a secondary matter. Under this regimen, the use of violence on a civilian target with intent to cause fear in a given civilian population is easily classified as a terrorist act.

In this light, bombings of public places, the sending of letter bombs or poisons through the mail, hijackings of aircraft, hostage taking, and so on, are all acts of terrorism regardless of the underlying cause said to justify the attack, or whether the attack occurs in peacetime or during war. Whatever the cause for the act, terrorism can simply be described as making "war" on civilians.

Still, a complete definition must also address the motive. Something must motivate the murderers that use terror. Shortly after 9/11, former United States Senator George Mitchell set his definition of terrorism under a political light: "Terrorism involves the deliberate killing of randomly selected noncombatants for political ends. It seeks to promote a political outcome by spreading terror and demoralization throughout a population." One can substitute Mitchell's word "political" with the word "religious" or the word "ideological" and the equation is still the same.

In summary, to the common understanding of the general public, terrorism is immediately associated with indiscriminate violence that is directed at innocent civilians in order to create a climate of fear which will cause an outcome (sometimes fear itself is the goal). The working definition that most civilized nations have adopted for their own domestic criminal code is patterned around four key characteristics of terrorism that better reflect the activity:

1. The illegal use of violence directed at civilians to produce fear in a target group.
2. The continuing threat of additional future acts of violence.
3. A predominately political, religious, or ideological character of the act.
4. The desire to mobilize or immobilize a given target group.

America's Definition of Terrorism

In the United States, the difficulties in definition are not related to a reluctance to use the term terrorism, but rather they rest in the sheer number of different government instrumentalities and federal statutes that have offered independent interpretations of terrorism which, while similar, are not identical. One of the best is found in Section 411 of the USA PATRIOT Act, which was signed into law with overwhelming bipartisan support in November of 2001.[8]

The USA PATRIOT Act provides similar definitions for "terrorist organization," "domestic terrorism," and "international terrorism." A terrorist organization is defined as one that is:

(1) designated by the Secretary of State as a terrorist organization under the process established under current law; (2) designated by the Secretary of State as a terrorist organization for immigration purposes; or (3) a group of two or more individuals that commits terrorist activities or plans or prepares to commit (including locating targets for) terrorist activities.

Domestic terrorism is defined in the USA PATRIOT Act with a slightly different emphasis. Domestic terrorism is the:

---

8. *See* The United and Strengthening America by Providing Appropriate Tools Required to Intercept and Obstruct Terrorism (U.S.A. PATRIOT) Act of 2001, Public Law Number 107-56, 115 Statute 272 (2001). The bill passed in the Senate by a vote of 98-1. 147 CONGRESSIONAL RECORD S11059-60 (2001). The House of Representatives passed their version by a vote of 357-66. 147 CONGRESSIONAL RECORD H7224 (2001).

> [U]nlawful use, or threatened use, of force or violence by a group or individuals based [in the United States] ... committed against persons or property to intimidate or coerce a government, [or] the civilian population ... in furtherance of political or social objectives.

International terrorism is set out in the USA PATRIOT Act as follows:

> International terrorism involves violent acts or acts dangerous to human life that violate the criminal laws of the United States or any state, or that would be a criminal violation if committed within the jurisdiction of the United States or any state. These acts appear intended to intimidate or coerce a civilian population, influence the policy of a government by intimidation or coercion, or affect the conduct of a government by assassination or kidnapping. International terrorist acts occur outside the United States or transcend national boundaries in terms of how terrorists accomplish them, the persons they appear intended to coerce or intimidate, or the place in which the perpetrators operate.

Terror is Goal Driven

Despite the lack of a fixed universal agreement defining terrorism, the essential goal of terrorism is readily identifiable. As the root word implies, the goal of terrorism is to instill fear in a given civilian population by means of violence. Sometimes, as with a criminal that uses terrorism to kill movie-goers in a theater, fear is the only goal. In most instances, the goal is broader—the resulting fear is supposed to cause a widespread action or reaction.

While specific acts of terrorism may appear to be mindless and irrational, terrorism is the exact opposite of confused behavior. Terrorism is a goal-directed, calculated, premeditated use of force.

All too often, terrorist tactics prove effective when those who are targeted respond in a way that reinforces the demands of the terrorists. For this reason, the official policy of the United States is not to negotiate with terrorists.

Two illustrations on this point. First, the March 11, 2004, coordinated train bombings in Spain by al-Qa'eda-linked terrorists not only killed 200 people, but the attacks caused the newly installed Spanish government to withdraw its military forces from the American-led coalition in Iraq, a coalition that was combating some of the very same forces of radical Islamic terror that attacked Spain.[9]

Second, the January 2015 terror attack by heavily armed radical Islamic terrorists in Paris achieved its goal of stifling free speech critical of Islam. Two brothers dispatched by al-Qa'eda in the Arabian Peninsula (AQAP) targeted the headquarters of the French satirical magazine *Charlie Hebdo* for its unflattering cartoon portrayals of the Prophet Muhammad. At the same time, keeping authorities on their toes, another Muslim jihadist targeted a Jewish kosher grocery store in Paris, killing four people.

When it was all over, the forces of radical Islam in the capital of France slaughtered seventeen innocent people that week. By the standard of the number of people killed, the Paris attacks were not significant when one considers the body count of radical Islam for the same week in January 2015 included some 2,000 murdered in Nigeria by the Islamist group Boko Haram and another 40 civilians murdered in Yemen by an al-Qa'eda car bomb (not counting the deaths of many hundreds of civilians by the Muslim group ISIS in Syria and Iraq).[10]

In response to the murders in Paris, on January 11, 2015, more than 40 world leaders led a march of one million people to show solidarity with the free speech expressions of the magazine. The world leaders boldly spoke out against the forces of radical Islam and the marchers proudly hoisted signs saying: " I am Charlie." Curiously, however, the rally only paraded in the non-Muslim neighborhoods in Paris and no muslim-led marches of any significance

---

9. Spain Train Bombings Fast Facts, CNN News, March 11, 2015, http://www.cnn.com/2013/11/04/world/europe/spain-train-bombings-fast-facts/index.html.
10. David Von Drehle, *The European Front*, Time, January 26, 2015, at 32.

occurred in the Muslim enclaves that surround Paris. The silence, where it was most needed, was deafening.

Most telling of all was how the civilized world responded when the next issue of *Charlie Hebdo* was published, with its cartoon of a crying Muhammad and the caption *"Je Suis Charlie"* (I am Charlie)" on the front cover.[11] Although several million copies were sold (normal sales are about 60,000), the majority of news outlets around the world that reported on the new publication refused to show the cover under the cowardly notion that anyone who dares offend radical Islam have only themselves to blame if they are killed for it. Despite the showy march and hoopla about free expression, the jihadists had achieved what they wanted. They had chilled free expression.

In turn, all across the Muslim world the reaction was headlined not on the jihadist hate crime but on condemning the new edition of *Charlie Hebdo* with Muhammad on the cover. One Muslim cleric in London called the new magazine cover of Muhammad an "act of war,"[12] because Islam forbids any portrayal of Muhammad.[13]

But sometimes the use of terror tactics can backfire on the perpetrators with unintended consequences. The al-Qa'eda terror group certainly did not seek the destruction of its primary base of operations in Taliban controlled Afghanistan when it attacked the United States on September 11, 2001. At most, al-Qa'eda hoped to spark a massive social and political revolution in the Middle East that would bring to power the ultra-conservative Islam called *salafism* (derived from *al salaf al salihal*—pious forefathers) across the Arab world and perhaps speed up the timetable for the creation of the next Muslim caliphate. As we shall see, ISIS was able to achieve the creation of the new caliphate, not al-Qa'eda.

---

11. *See* Maya Vidon, *Charlie Hebdo is a Can't-Get Must-Have*, USA TODAY, January 15, 2015, at A1.
12. Jacob Resneck & Mal Shams El-Din, *Charlie Backlash is Swift Among Muslims*, USA TODAY, January 15, 2015, at A7.
13. *See* Carol Kuruvilla, *Does Islam Really Forbid Images of Muhammad?* THE HUFFINGTON POST, January 8, 2015.

Weapons of Mass Destruction

Over three quarters of all international terror groups are tied into the religion of radical Islam as their chief criterion and motivator for action. In 2014, the State Department's list of foreign terrorist organizations included 45 of 59, or 76 percent of known, active, international terrorist groups, as predominately associated with radical Islam.[14] This is a significant spike from previous official reports where radical Islam represented less than 50 percent.

The greatest fear in the context of radical Islam and terrorism is their eventual acquisition of a weapon of mass destruction (WMD).[15] Apart from the traditional weapons used by terrorists, one must now add WMD as a special definitional subset. Although current federal statutes take an extremely broad view of what constitutes a WMD (to include a pipe bomb), an early and still relevant definition comes from Section 1403 of the National Defense Authorization Act for fiscal year 1997. WMD are not the small things, they are the stuff of nightmares:

> [A]ny weapon or device that is intended, or has the capability, to cause death or serious bodily injury to a significant number of people through the release of toxic or poisonous chemicals or their precursors, a disease organism, or radiation or radioactivity.[16]

In its broadest sense, WMD include not only nuclear material, but the full range of biological, chemical, and radioactive agents. A true WMD event kills in the hundreds of thousands, perhaps mil-

14. Foreign Terrorist Organizations (FTOs) are designated by the Secretary of State in accordance with section 219 of the Immigration and Nationality Act (INA).

15. *National Strategy to Combat Weapons of Mass Destruction*, NSPD-17/HSPD 4 (Dec. 2002) [unclassified version] (describing the U.S. strategy utilizing counter-proliferation, non-proliferation, and consequence management to address the threat of use of Weapons of Mass Destruction (WMD) against the United States.

16. Defense Against Weapons of Mass Destruction Act, National Authorization Act for FY 1997, Title XIV, Pub. L. No. 104-201 (September 23, 1996).

lions. Radical Islam would like nothing better than to use them for
the sole purpose of removing all infidels from the earth. It is entirely possible that one day in the not too distant future America will
awaken to the gut wrenching news headlines of: "Chicago Gone,"
"New York No More," or "Washington Wiped Off The Map."

A December 2008 Congressionally mandated report by the
Commission on the Prevention of Weapons of Mass Destruction
Proliferation and Terrorism understood the mindset of radical Islam
and the use of WMD,[17] even if their predicted date for such an attack (2013) was off.

> Terrorists [radical Islamists] are determined to attack us
> again with weapons of mass destruction if they can. Osama
> bin Laden has said that obtaining these weapons is a "re-
> ligious duty" and is reported to have sought to perpetrate
> another "Hiroshima." The Commission believes that un-
> less the world community acts decisively and with great
> urgency, it is more likely than not that a weapon of mass
> destruction will be used in a terrorist attack somewhere in
> the world by 2013.[18]

It is not if radical Islam can, it is when they will.

States & Terrorism

As is true for any terrorist event, there are three general sources from
which a terrorist attack can emanate—States, sub-State groups, or
individuals. States that engage in terrorism are further divided as
either State-sponsors or State-supporters of terrorism. Tragically,
in the so-called information age, all three categories have demon-

---

17. *National Strategy to Combat Weapons of Mass Destruction*, NSPD-
17/HSPD 4 (December 2002) [unclassified version] (describing the U.S.
strategy utilizing counter-proliferation, non-proliferation, and consequence
management to address the threat of use of Weapons of Mass Destruction
(WMD) against the United States and its friends and allies).
18. Bob Graham, Jim Talent, & Graham T. Allison, WORLD AT RISK: THE REPORT
OF THE COMMISSION ON THE PREVENTION OF WMD PROLIFERATION AND TERRORISM
(2008).

strated a willingness to use terror tactics in the physical world and there can be no doubt that this thirst for unlawful violence will soon spill over in a dramatic fashion into the cyber world as well.

Perhaps the most easily identifiable category of terrorism is the State-sponsored terrorist. Each year the U.S. State Department designates certain countries as State sponsors of terrorism for repeatedly providing "support for international acts of terrorism."[19] This list generally includes a small handful of States that has in the past included: North Korea, Libya, Cuba, Iran, Iraq, Sudan, and Syria. Currently, only Iran, Sudan, and Syria remain on the list.[20] The Bush Administration removed North Korea, Libya, and Iraq and the Obama Administration removed Cuba from the list. Syria is now a failed State, but Iran is the one mainstay on the list and still remains as the number one State-sponsor of terrorism. The puppet master of State-sponsored terrorism, Iran has operatives on every continent.

State-sponsored terrorism exists when a State directly uses its own resources to sponsor acts of terrorism against other people or nations. Since accountability for such acts are most often denied, the aggressor-State generally avoids responsibility. Of course, with Iran this is not the case. Iran openly boasts of supporting terrorist groups like Hezbollah in Lebanon and Hamas in the Palestinian territories. Iran also has close ties with the socialist regime of Venezuela as well as North Korea and Russia.

A classic case of a State-sponsored act of terrorism occurred in 1986 when Libyan government agents bombed an American frequented discotheque in Berlin, Germany. This secretive act of terror was followed by a second State-sponsored act of terror in 1988, when Libyan government operatives bombed Pan Am Flight 103 over Lockerbie, Scotland, killing all 278 people on board.

In contrast to the State-sponsored scenario, the State-supported terrorist group generally operates in a more independent fashion from the host State. State-supported terrorism refers to the practice of a State providing resources or finances to a terrorist group for

---

19. *See* State Sponsors of Terrorism, United States Department of State, 22 U.S.C. 2656f.
20. *Id.*

training and logistics. This occurred in Afghanistan prior to 2001, where the terrorist group then headed by Osama bin Laden once took open refuge. The host State is not directly involved; the Taliban government did not attack America on 9/11, al-Qa'eda did.

In terms of culpability, it is difficult to make a practical distinction between State-sponsored and State-supported terrorism. The terms really speak only to the degree of involvement. If the rule of law has any validity, States that knowingly allow terrorist groups to operate with impunity on their soil should never be able to escape the attendant lawful consequences.

The final category of terrorism in reference to a State is the sub-State terrorist organization. Sub-State terrorist groups can either be domestic or international terrorist organizations. These terror groups do not operate with the approval or sponsorship of the host nation. The host nation may know that the group exists in name, but has no actionable knowledge that the group is providing material support to terrorist groups or engaging in terrorist activities.

Like ticks on a dog, there are many sub-State terror groups that operate in many nations around the world and in the United States. As will be addressed, in the United States they can be further distinguished as right-wing groups, left-wing groups, or radical Islamic groups.

Regardless of the type of sub-State terror group the paramount concern in the modern era is their use of a WMD. The first significant use of a quasi-WMD by a sub-State group occurred on March 20, 1995, when members of the Aum Shinrikyo religious cult (now called Aleph) in Japan released a lethal nerve agent, sarin, in a Tokyo underground subway. This gas attack killed twelve people and injured 3,000 others, clearly demonstrating that the scenario of terrorists using a real WMD was not the stuff of science fiction.

The radical Islamic group ISIS has also used poison mustard gas against Peshmerga Kurdish fighters in Syria in 2015. Captured from Syrian military sites, even in low doses, the poison gas fills the airways slowly suffocating its victim.[21]

---

21. Adam Entous, *ISIS Suspect of Chemical Attack*, WALL STREET JOURNAL, August 14, 2015, at A1.

Lone-wolf Terrorism

The accurate identification of the lone-wolf terrorist describes the situation where an individual acts alone when he engages in terror without any affiliation to another person, group, or ideology. Most often, these individuals are arrogant criminals suffering from a mental illness who have a lust in their souls to terrorize the innocent. Because these individuals have no group identification they are harder to predict, track, or deter.

There are many examples of lone-wolf terrorists ranging from those that murder innocent movie-goers to those that murder children in schools. Two examples will suffice to illustrate the category.

The 2001 anthrax-tainted letter attacks that killed five people and traumatized the nation was said to have been carried out by an anthrax researcher at the U.S. Army's biodefense laboratory in Maryland. After a massive investigation lasting almost seven years, the prime suspect, Bruce Ivins, committed suicide in July 2008 as federal authorities were closing in to formally arrest him.

Like all lone-wolf terrorists, Ivins was an arrogant criminal who used the tactic of terrorism to satisfy his degenerate lusts. Interestingly, Ivins, a middle aged white male, tried to portray himself as a Muslim terrorist writing in his letters phrases such as "Praise Allah" and "Death to America." He was nothing of the kind.

Another horrendous example of a lone-wolf attack occurred in 2015 in Charleston, South Carolina, when Dylann Roof murdered 9 black Americans in a church. While the accused was a mentally ill self-proclaimed white supremacist, he was not tied in to any organization and acted entirely alone.

Interestingly, this act of terrorism not only aroused the same old liberal mantra about gun control but it also sparked a knee jerk reaction to identify the Confederate battle flag with hate and racism. Within hours of the murders ideologues and their propagandists resurrected the false narrative that the Southern Cross (the name for the battle flag) stands for white racism and must be purged from America.[22] The fault for the murders rested more so with the Con-

---

22. *See* Miriam Rozen, *The History or Hate Debate*, Texas Lawyer, July 13, 2005.

federate flag than with the mentally ill killer. This false *ad populum* (appeal to the people) argument equating the Confederate battle flag to racism—"Southerners fly the rebel flag because they hate"—is naked demagoguery, but it succeeded in spurring politicians to blatantly remove the rebel flag which had long flown on the Confederate war memorials in Columbia, South Carolina and in Montgomery, Alabama. No referendum on removal of the flag was offered to the people of South Carolina or Alabama because the politicians knew that ¾ of its citizens would have voted NO.[23]

While it is true that some racists misuse the Confederate Battle flag for their own nefarious purposes—along with the Christian cross and the American flag—it is not true that the majority of white Southerners are racists or that the Confederacy was any more racist than the Northern States they resisted when invaded in 1861.

Sadly, one can argue from a point of perfect logic that the historical facts demonstrate quite plainly that the War Between the States was not about slavery, although slavery ended because of the War; that slavery was an American sin that enriched the North and South alike, not a Confederate sin; that racism was just as rampant in the North as in the South, de facto segregation vs. de jure segregation; that Lincoln freed zero slaves with his politically motivated Emancipation Proclamation, he was in fact a bigot himself who strongly supported the American Colonization Society (Lincoln wanted all freed blacks sent to West Africa or Central America); that the Southern icon General Robert E. Lee freed all his slaves during the War, he was opposed to slavery and supported gradual manumission; that the majority of Southerners did not own slaves, the Confederate soldier fought because the South was invaded by vast federal armies; that the heritage group the Sons of Confederate Veterans has black members, black Southerners fought with the South, etc., until blue in the face, but it will do no good.[24] The

23. *Id.* Some politicians and community leaders from Southern States that did not have a Confederate flag flying at a War memorial turned instead to attacking all things Confederate to include street names, school names, grave memorials, park names, etc.
24. FORGOTTEN CONFEDERATES: AN ANTHOLOGY ABOUT BLACK SOUTHERNERS, Charles Kelly Barrow, J.H. Segars & R. B. Rosenburg (1995).

forces of "presentism," a new political correctness vetting process which "mercilessly subjects history and historical figures to a contemporary social enlightenment," cares nothing for context, common sense, or truth.[25]

It is also safe to say that opponents to the Southern battle flag also realize something else that deeply upsets them when they see it flying freely in the breeze. They understand that the rebel flag is a universal symbol of resistance to tyranny and at the same time a symbol of devotion to the principles of limited government and States rights—hateful concepts to those on the political left. Considering the unprecedented expansion of the federal government in modern America, many believe it is time to raise the Confederate flag in defiance, not lower it.

In any event, in the context of the use of terror, the vicious act of one mentally ill murderer had tremendous repercussions. Dylann Roof was a criminal but also qualified as a lone-wolf terrorist. His act of terror greatly assisted those who promote the view that the rebel flag stands for racism and worked against those who view the Southern Cross as a symbol of heritage and admiration for the prowess and sacrifice of the Confederate soldier.[26]

So, what causes the Ivins' and Roof's of this world to terrorize the innocent? Ultimately, it matters little how a person is raised, their soul is their own. In his ground-breaking book on criminal behavior, entitled *Inside the Criminal Mind*, Dr. Stanton E. Samenow, Jr., summed it all up quite succinctly: *criminals cause crime*.

> Criminals cause crime—not bad neighborhoods, inadequate
> parents, television, schools, drugs, or unemployment. Crime

25. Ross. K. Baker, *Voices: Democrats Foolishly Purge Heroes*, USA TODAY, August 11, 2015, at A2.
26. With over 30,000 members, the Sons of Confederate Veterans was organized in 1896 and is "a historical, patriotic, and non-political organization" to honor the valor of the Confederate soldier. Membership is open to all male descendants of any veteran who served honorably in the Confederate armed forces. *See* http://www.scv.org. The United States Combined Federal Campaign (CFC) includes the Sons of Confederate Veterans as a qualified CFC charity, number 10116 on the 2015 CGC list.

resides in the minds of human beings and is not caused by social conditions. Once we as a society recognize this simple fact, we shall take measures radically different from current ones. To be sure, we shall continue to remedy intolerable social conditions for this is worthwhile in and of itself. But we shall not expect criminals to change because of such efforts.[27]

Finally, what about the jihadist as a lone-wolf terrorist? President Obama was always quick at press conferences to refer to a single Muslim jihadist who committed terror on their own as just a "lone-wolf." In this manner he tried to marginalize the threat of radical Islam here in America, and hoped that no one would notice the logical fallacy. To call a jihadist merely a lone-wolf terrorist is beyond fuzzy thinking, it is an *ad ignorantiam* appeal to today's ill-informed populace. A single jihadist acting alone in a terror attack does not fit the definition of a lone-wolf terrorist. They may do the act of terror by themselves, but they are tied in to the exact same mindset as the multitudes of other radical Islamists around the world. They may never meet each other in person, but they see eye-to-eye in their desire for *jihad-fee-sabeelillah*, (martyrdom for the cause of Allah) in order to conquer the world for Islam. More on this later.

Sub-State Terrorist Types in America
Apart from the State-sponsor, State-supporter, or lone-wolf criminal that engages in terrorism, there are three general types of sub-State terror groups that have used the tactic of terrorism in America. These are right-wing extremists, left-wing extremists, and radical Islamic extremists. Because, far and away, radical Islam constitutes the biggest threat as a sub-State terror hate group they will be covered as a separate matter in Chapter 8.

Let's first address right-wing extremists. Upon taking office in 2009, one of the first things that the Obama Administration did was to place great emphasis on right-wing extremism in America

27. Stanton E. Samenow, Jr., INSIDE THE CRIMINAL MIND 6 (1984).

as a way to disguise the far more serious threat of radical Islam and perhaps to cast derision on conservatives at the same time. The Department of Homeland Security (DHS) issued a report that not only labeled as right-wing extremists those individuals who are: (1) hate-oriented towards non-white minorities; and (2) entertain an extreme dislike for centralized federal government authority, but also cautioned law enforcement to be aware of other categories of Americans that needed to be "watched." Incredibly, the DHS cited: (1) returning military combat veterans; (2) those dissatisfied with the manner in which the federal government is handling the security of the Southern border; and (3) people that inordinately embrace limited government, to be ripe for recruitment by right-wing extremist groups.[28]

Of course, conservatives in America fall into one or more of these DHS categories that bear "watching." I actually fulfill all three: (1) I am a 20 year veteran of the U.S. Army and have received combat pay on four different occasions; (2) I believe our Southern border is about as secure as a screen door on a submarine, and (3) I fully embrace limited government.

In lock step with President Obama's clear desire to take the spotlight off of radical Islam and the War on Terror, most so-called advocacy watch groups such as the Southern Poverty Law Center are more than happy to continue their long standing policy of fixating on right-wing groups and generally ignoring altogether left-wing groups and radical Islam. Engaging in selective *bias by labeling*, they remain quick to attach the "hate" label to right-wing extremist groups, but never to left-wing groups or radical Islam. And sometimes they attach the label to conservative groups that simply embrace conservative principles or heritage rights.

It is true that right-wing hate groups that employ terror exist in the United States, but it is absolutely not true that they are the primary source of terror attacks on American soil. It is also true that the Constitutional right of free speech protects right-wing hate

---

28. U.S. Department of Homeland Security Assessment, Rightwing Extremism: Current Economic and Political Climate Fueling Resurgence in Radicalization and Recruitment (2009), *available at* http://www.fas.org/irp/eprint/rightwing. pdf.

groups just as it protects any other type of hate group so long as that group does not violate State or federal criminal codes. In short, anyone in America has the right to hold bizarre opinions, hateful opinions, and intolerant opinions.

On the other hand, where there is smoke, there is likely to be fire at some point. All hate groups and people that spew hate bear watching. When anyone uses violence, aides and abets in violence, conspires to use violence, solicits others to violence, or provides material support to terrorism they are subject to criminal sanctions.

So what is a right-wing extremist? Right-wing extremists are generally referred to as those who have an extreme hypersensitivity or paranoia to centralized government, usually at the federal level, but the term also includes racists and bigots that embrace a racial or religious based hatred towards others.

The most notorious example of a right-wing terrorist attack in the United States occurred in April 1995 with the car bombing of the Murrah Federal Building in Oklahoma City by Timothy McVeigh.[29] McVeigh held bizarre anti-federal government sentiments that he manifested by the bombing which also killed 167 people, including women and children. McVeigh viewed the civilian deaths as "collateral damage."

Although certain biased progressives on the left seek to paint all conservatives as right-wing extremists, there is a vast difference between a conservative and a right-wing extremist. In reality, right-wing extremists have little to do with the conservative American who embraces the simple principles of "God, guns, and limited government" and holds as anathema the increasing intrusion of federal authority in their lives.

In summary, right-wing extremists can range from anti-government militia organizations, to white supremacist groups like the

29. See Michael A. Newton, *Exceptional Engagement: Protocol I and A World United Against Terrorism*, 45 TEXAS INTERNATIONAL LAW JOURNAL 323, 343 n.92 (2009) (citing Edward F. Mickolus et al., INTERNATIONAL TERRORISM IN THE 1980s: VOLUME II 1984–1987 XIII (1989) ("Right-wing terrorism refers to acts perpetrated by outlawed groups that do not seek a social revolution but resort to violence as a way to express and advance their political goals, such as ultra-nationalism and anticommunism.").

Aryan Brotherhood or the Ku Klux Klan. Although not always the case, right-wing extremists like McVeigh, generally target symbols of federal authority when they engage in terrorism.[30]

At the other end of the spectrum are left-wing extremists. Left-wing extremists are generally characterized by hyper egalitarian-ism, hatred of nationalism, opposition to free market capitalism, and opposition to the armed forces.[31] Some are lured into the flock as an overreaction to real of perceived white-collar crime. Despite the fact that God recognizes capitalism and the private ownership of property as legitimate, "thou shalt not steal," leftists assume it to be wrong and eagerly embrace utopian socialism as the preferred alternative. While evil practices will occur in capitalism, socialism is inherently evil. Other left-wing extremists are simply anarchists.

Like its counterpart on the far right, left-wing extremism also includes bigots that despise all who do not share their ideals. They seek to eradicate most of the tried and true societal norms related to marriage, family, business, and nationalism.

Other left-wing groups like the Earth Liberation Front are la-beled as eco-terrorists and are characterized by an extreme dedi-cation to protecting the so-called natural environment. Eco-terror-ism targets with violence businesses and government agencies they perceive as engaging in actions that disrupt or harm the environ-ment.[32]

Just as conservatives are not right-wing extremists, liberals are not left-wing extremists. For example, liberals who strongly advo-cate for increased power to the federal government, may sympa-thize with some portions of left-wing extremist ideology but few

---

30. In 2015, self-professed member of the Ku Klux Klan, Glendon Craw-ford, of Galway, New York, was convicted in federal court for attempting to use a radiological device to kill Muslims in New York. *See*

31. *See* Brent L. Smith, TERRORISM IN AMERICA: PIPE BOMBS AND PIPE DREAMS 24-25 (1994).

32. *See* Rebecca K. Smith, *"Ecoterrorism"?: A Critical Analysis of the Vilification of Radical Environmental Activists As Terrorists*, 38 ENVIRONMEN-TAL LAW 537, 545-46 (2008). *See also* Joshua K. Marquis & Danielle M. Weiss, *Eco-Terror: Special Interest Terrorism*, PROSECUTOR, Jan. 2005, at 30 (discussing the underground radical eco-terrorist group, The Earth Libera-tion Front).

would argue for destroying all vestiges of States rights or capitalism.

When the left-wing extremist turns to violence, they often target symbols of capitalism to include animal research facilities. The "Unabomber" Ted Kaczynski is a prime example of a left-wing extremist. Highly educated, Kaczynski was a nature-centered leftist who was vehemently opposed to industrialization and capitalism. During the course of several years he sent numerous letter bombs to those that promoted modern technology, killing three and injuring over 20.[33]

A more recent illustration of left-wing extremism occurred during the "Occupy Wall-Street" protests where thousands of radical leftists destroyed and vandalized public and private property in several cities in the U.S. to rail against capitalism. Amazingly, both State and federal authorities did very little to break up the illegal squatter camps that sprang up on public property in the downtown areas of large cities.

---

33. Glaberson, William, *Lawyers Drop Mental Defense for Kaczynski*, N. Y. Times, December 29, 1997, at A1.

Chapter 2

The War on Terror

"All that is necessary for evil to triumph is for good men to do nothing."[1]

—Edmund Burke

Some have tried to depict the War on Terror as a war against all of Islam. This is simply not true. In its broadest sense, the War on Terror is a term that describes the ongoing conflict against all those Muslims who embrace a highly radicalized Islam—a view of Islam that encourages and directs aggressive violence against the United States of America as well as all who do not share their view of Islam, what the jihadists call the true Islam. In point of fact, the followers of radical Islam have killed more Muslims than Christians or Jews.

The war was started by the forces of radical Islam, not by the United States. In 1996, Osama bin Laden, the founder of al-Qa'eda, issued his first declaration that he was at war with the United States. But the key declaration of war from the perspective of radical Islam was made on February 22, 1998, when Osama bin Laden and the "World Islamic Front" formally issued a Muslim religious *fatwa* requiring all Muslims to engage in physical violence, jihad, against

---

1.   America's God and Country Encyclopedia of Quotations 82 (1994).

"Crusaders [Americans] and Jews." Signed by Sheikh (a Muslim scholar) Osama bin-Muhammed bin Laden, Ayman al Zawahiri, Abu-Yasir Rifa'i Ahmad Taha, Sheikh Mir Hamzah, and Fazlur Rahman, the declaration proclaimed:

> All these crimes and sins committed by the Americans are a clear declaration of war on Allah, his messenger, and Muslims. And *ulema* [clerics] have throughout Islamic history unanimously agreed that jihad is an individual duty if the enemy destroys Muslim countries. On that basis, and in compliance with Allah's order, we issue the following fatwa to all Muslims: The ruling to kill the Americans and their allies—civilians and military—is an individual duty for every Muslim who can do it in any country in which it is possible to do it, in order to liberate the al-Aqsa Mosque [in Jerusalem] and the holy mosque [Mecca] from their grip.[2]

Although al-Qa'eda had been at war for several years with America, America did not enter the War on Terror until September 11, 2001, when 19 members of the radical Islamic terror group al-Qa'eda hijacked four U.S. passenger aircraft while in flight to conduct simultaneous attacks. The operation had been methodically planned and financed from al-Qa'eda "central" in Afghanistan.[3] The targets for the terror strikes were carefully selected as the three prominent pillars of the United States of America—the heart of the financial district in New York, the heart of our military headquarters in the Pentagon, and the heart of the federal government in Washington D.C.

Four U.S. passenger planes full of innocent civilians were hijacked and used in a spectacular terror attack with the 19 Islamists divided into four terror squads. Five jihadists were assigned to overpower the flight personnel in each of three planes with a squad of four jihadists for the fourth jetliner (the so-called 20th hijacker,

---

2.   Peter L. Bergen, THE OSAMA BIN LADEN I KNOW 196 (2006).
3.   *See* 9/11 COMMISSION REPORT: FINAL REPORT OF THE NATIONAL COMMISSION ON TERRORIST ATTACKS UPON THE UNITED STATES 51 (2004).

Moussaoui, was later captured and prosecuted in federal court).[4]

The jihadists intentionally crashed two of the planes into the Twin Towers of the World Trade Center in New York City.[5] A third plane was crashed into the Pentagon in Washington, D.C. Among the dead in the Pentagon attack was the husband of my former secretary who worked with me when I was assigned as the Deputy Chief of the Army's International & Operational Law Division at the Pentagon. The fourth high-jacked plane went down in an open field in Pennsylvania, most likely as a result of the heroic efforts of some of the passengers. Along with billions of dollars in property loss, 3,000 people were horribly murdered, not including the radical Islamist terrorists. Thus, began the War on Terror.

On its face, the phrase War on Terror is rather confusing but it is undeniably a catchy one and has proven to be quite resilient over the past decade and a half. Coined by President Bush on the day of 9/11, but unofficially banned by President Obama when he took office in 2009,[6] it has nevertheless survived intact. Over the years, it has been used both as a metaphor to describe a general conflict against all international Islamist terror groups and also in a more precise sense to describe the lawful combat operations against the radical Islamist organizations the Taliban and al-Qa'eda. The phrase was also disingenuously invoked by the Bush Administration to help explain the need for the combat operation which crushed Saddam Hussein's military in 2003.

From a black letter law perspective, the most correct use of the term is to describe the ongoing international armed conflict between the United States of America and the "Taliban, al-Qa'eda, or

---

4. Evan Thomas, *A New Date of Infamy*, Newsweek, Sept. 13, 2001, at 22 (setting out a detailed timeline of the events that took place on September 11, 2001).

5. *See Terrorists Destroy World Trade Center, Hit Pentagon in Raid With Hijacked Jets*, Wall Street Journal, September 12, 2001, at A1.

6. Obama coined his own phrase called "Overseas Contingency Operations." This phrase was first used in a memo to Pentagon staff members in late March 2009, which stated: "This administration prefers to avoid using the term 'Long War' or 'Global War on Terror.' Please use 'Overseas Contingency Operation.'" Scott Wilson & Al Kamen, *"Global War on Terror" is Given New Name*, Washington Post, March 25, 2009, at A4.

associated forces."[7] This descriptive phraseology is taken from the 2006 Military Commissions Act (MCA). Coupled with the 2001 Authorization for Use of Military Force, the MCA is perhaps the clearest of all the various Congressional pronouncements for war and consequently for the use of the rule of law known as the law of war. The MCA lists "unlawful enemy combatants" as:

> (i) a person who has engaged in hostilities or who has purposefully and materially supported hostilities against the United States or its co-belligerents who is not a lawful enemy combatant (including a person who is part of the *Taliban, al Qaeda* [sic], or *associated forces*); or ....

The most pointed complaint about the phrase War on Terror is that it is woefully non-descriptive. Although the War on Terror validates the fact that there is a war, it does not tell you who the enemy is. As already noted, however, since the MCA identifies for the public the actual enemies in the War on Terror, this matter could be remedied quite easily. A better term for the now longest war in American history would be the *Taliban, al-Qa'eda, and Associated Forces War*. But, of course, that phrase is too long, so we simply stick with the term War on Terror.

In and of itself this is not that unusual, as Americans do have a penchant for shorting the names of our many wars. For instance, the term World War II is very non-descriptive. To be precise one would have to label that war as *Nazi Germany, Imperialist Japan, and Fascist Italy War*.[8] Too long. We just call it World War II and assume that everyone can mentally fill in the blank as to the identity of the enemy forces.

---

7. *See* Military Commissions Act of 2006, Public Law Number 109-366, 120 Statute 2600, 10 U.S.C. § 948 (2006).

8. *See generally* Harold Evans, THE AMERICAN CENTURY (1998). During World War II (1939-1945), a large group of the world's nations banded together to form what was formally known as the Allied Powers, in an effort to combat the Axis Powers. The Allies included the United States, the United Kingdom, the Soviet Union, China, France, Poland, Greece, Canada, Yugoslavia, Czechoslovakia, Australia, New Zealand, India, Egypt, and Brazil, as well as many other countries.

Thus, the main point of the War on Terror is that it uses the word "war." Historically, all labels for all wars that America has fought have included the word "war." This is a fundamental ingredient that provides the clearest signal that the nation is using the law of war and not operating outside the rule of law. In other words, this is a real war that entitles the United States to operate under the rule of law "toolbox" called the law of war and not exclusively under the rule of law "toolbox" called domestic criminal law. Even though the enemy in this war are non-State actors and not the traditional nation-state, it is entirely appropriate and lawful to kill them on site, detain them indefinitely, and use military commissions to prosecute those charged with war crimes.

As such, Obama's first Secretary of Homeland Security, Janet Napolitano, was grossly inaccurate and disingenuous when she remarked that Obama wanted to purge the phrase "War on Terror" because "[i]n some respects 'war' is too limiting."[9] Without question, the truth is the exact opposite. The use of the law of war expands, not restricts, the available legal powers necessary to deal with certain elements of radical Islam. The only real truth is that Obama was consistent in his relentless desire to ban the War on Terror for political purposes.

Confusion on the Home front

While the above analysis of both the term and legality of the War on Terror seems rather straightforward, the reality is that vast numbers of Americans remain in a perpetual state of confusion when it comes to discerning basic facts about how America conducts itself in the War on Terror. Allegations of illegality are as common as dirt. The main reason for the confusion rests not with the complexity of the concepts but rather with the role that American politics plays in the process.

---

9. *See* Daniel Dombey & Edward Luce, *'Global War on Terror' Out of Lexicon*, FINANCIAL TIMES (London), June 30, 2009, at 4 (quoting Secretary of Homeland Security Janet Napolitano, who confirmed that "War on Terror" is not used because it "does not describe properly the nature of the terrorist threat to the US").

Here then is the situation that spawns the demagogue and confusion. Our nation has two main political parties, Republican and Democratic. Each political party desires to take control of the executive and congressional branches of government so that they can implement their own policies. So when the Republican party is in control, the Democratic party will not heap praise on how wonderful the Republicans are performing, and *vice versa*.

When 9/11 occurred the Republican party was in control of the executive branch and held it until January 2009. During much of this period Democrats with the assistance of many liberals in the news media kept up a steady bombardment of complaint and disinformation about almost everything that President Bush did or attempted to do, e.g., the PATRIOT Act was evil and illegal; the military run dentition facility at Guantanamo Bay, Cuba (GITMO), was a hell hole and violated human rights; the military commissions were unconstitutional; the war in Iraq was based on intentional lies and deception by Republicans; the war in Afghanistan was illegal and poorly handled; drone attacks were unconstitutional; the Bush Administration was secretly torturing detainees wholesale at Abu Ghraib; the military regularly committed war crimes against Muslim women and children; and so on.

To be sure, the shrill voices of discontent about the War on Terror are extant today, but the hysteria was extreme during the Bush Administration with an overly obsessive fixation on the U.S. military run detention facility at GITMO. Constructive criticism is one thing, but the mantra of repeated falsehoods of *bias by commission* (presenting only one side of an issue) and *bias by omission* (ignoring facts that tend to disprove claims) poisoned the atmosphere of honest inquiry to the point where few could comprehend even the basic precepts of international or domestic law. In short, the disinformation campaign worked!

Even today, when I am asked to deliver a speech on some aspect of terrorism, I generally begin my remarks by throwing out a short quiz to the audience in order to vividly demonstrate that they have been sold a false bill of goods by those who have made it a cottage industry to demonize America's conduct in the War on Terror.

Admittedly there are dozens of popular misconceptions that I could choose from to illustrate my point, but my all-time favorite challenge is about GITMO and "water-boarding."

I pose three short fact based questions: (1) "Was any detainee at GITMO every water-boarded?;" (2) "Has the military, regardless of the geographic location, ever water-boarded any of the thousands of detainees taken to date in the War on Terror?" (to include the thousands detained by President Obama in Afghanistan); and (3) "How many detainees were actually water-boarded?"

In the hundreds of speeches I have made all over the world, every single audience, foreign or domestic, flunks the quiz by a large margin. The general consensus about GITMO goes something like this: "If it's Thursday, it's time for the military guards to drag out a dozen or so detainees by their beards and water-board the hell out of them."

When I provide the real fact based answers the audience is dumbfounded: (1) No detainee was ever water-boarded at GITMO—zero; (2) The military has never water-boarded a single detainee—zero; and (3) only three high-value radical Islamist detainees were ever water-boarded in the past 15 plus years (the US Justice Department approved program only lasted from 2002-2004) and that under the auspices of the CIA at an off-shore location(s).

Next, I ask a follow up question: "If you, as an intelligent cross section of people, have consumed the "Kool-Aid" of disinformation about GITMO and waterboarding, what chance does the average uninformed person have to discern the truth about any of the myriad topics of contention?" None—zero.

While upsetting the apple cart of nonsense spooned out by the far left's vilification of the War on Terror is amusing, the real fun in confronting this vast disinformation campaign is when I get to engage their high priests—the leading educators and journalists—in public debate. The staunch adherents and chief propagandists of disinformation about the War on Terror fill the halls of academia, government, and the mainstream media. As one of only a few conservative law professors in the nation, I have debated many of these leaders to include my fellow law professors at law schools and other forums from here to "ten buck two" (Timbuktu is a city in West Africa).

Whatever the topic of contention, be it the PATRIOT Act or nuclear nonproliferation, I always conclude my remarks by posing a final question to my opponent: "In the light of your criticism voiced here today, what recommendations would you make to the appropriate branch of government or industry to fix the problem?" In each and every case they retort that they have no recommendations at all—they desire to remain neutral! I, of course, do not wish to remain neutral. I am an American and I want to win!

On the political side of things, I offer two very fascinating illustrations of the confusion. The first is related to sworn testimony to Congress and the second is a one-on-one debate with the head of the American Civil Liberties Union (ACLU).

Along with three other law professors from across the United States I was asked in 2008 to provide sworn testimony as a subject matter expert before a "fact finding" hearing called by the majority Democratic *Senate Committee on the Judiciary, Subcommittee on Administrative Oversight and the Courts*. Obviously a political hatchet job against Republicans and the Bush Administration over the waterboarding of three high-value detainees, the hearing was blatantly entitled: *"What Went Wrong, Torture and the Office of the Legal Counsel in the Bush Administration."*[10] To observe that the Senate was not exactly using our tax dollars to conduct a fair and balanced fact-finding mission is an understatement.

Out of the four law professors asked for their professional legal opinions regarding whether or not torture occurred in the interrogation process, I was the only law professor to testify that the waterboarding technique used and approved by the Justice Department did not rise to the level of "severe pain and suffering" as defined by the Torture Convention.[11] Based on leading international case

---

10. *What Went Wrong: Torture and the Office of the Legal Counsel in the Bush Administration: Hearing Before the S. Comm. on the Judiciary*, 111th Cong. (2009) (statement of Dr. Jeffrey F. Addicott, Professor of Law, Center for Terrorism Law, St. Mary's University School of Law), http://judiciary.senate.gov/hearings/testimony.cfm?id=3842&wit_id=7904.
11. Convention Against Torture and Other Cruel, Inhuman or Degrading

law such as *Ireland vs. United Kingdom*,[12] I testified that the United States had never officially engaged in torture, not even close (I did not address abuses by government officials that had engaged in torture or murder in their individual capacity). I did, however, point out to the Democratic Senators that faced me that day that I believed that they had most certainly violated the Torture Convention because they refused to call for criminal prosecutions as required by Article 7 of the Convention, if they believed that torture had occurred.[13] For this I was roundly protested by a large contingent of females from the leftist "Code Pink" group in the back of the hearing room.

The second illustration of the confusion on the home front involves a most memorable debate that took place at the prestigious University of Pittsburgh School of Law, in Pittsburgh, Pennsylvania in 2010. I was cordially invited to engage in a one-on-one verbal "shoot out" with the President of the ACLU, Susan Herman, a law professor at New York University School of Law. The topic was *Terrorism, Rights, and National Security*. As one would expect, the audience of well over a hundred consisted of people who had come out of the woodwork from various ACLU sub-units around the northeast. I am sure these elitists had come to watch the triumph of "reason and social justice" by their supreme leader.

Professor Herman won the coin toss as to the order of presentation and being a shrewd debater she elected to go second (letting your opponent go first is always preferable as it allows you to listen to the opposing side's argument and then craft your remarks accordingly). Of course, this tactic failed miserably, primarily because I

Treatment or Punishment, G.A. Res. 39/46, U.N. GAOR, 39th Sess., Supp. No. 51 at 197, United Nation Document A/39/51 (December 10, 1984) (setting forth the standards of treatment for all persons and the universal rejection of "torture and other cruel, inhuman or degrading treatment or punishment throughout the world"). The convention provides a clear definition of torture, although it is lacking any definition of "other cruel, inhuman or degrading treatment."

12. *Id.*

13. The text can be viewed in entirety at: http://jurist.law.pitt.edu/paperchase/2009/05/bush-era-interrogation-techniques.php.

already knew what Professor Herman was going to say. Liberals are very predictable.

Her premise was that the War on Terror did not qualify as a real war under international or domestic law and therefore America's actions were grossly illegal. The indefinite detention of individuals at GITMO without criminal charges was unconstitutional, killing unarmed "enemy combatants" was murder, and military commissions were an outrage and human rights violation. In short, America was "shredding the US Constitution and international law."

I opened with the frank acknowledgement that if the War on Terror was not a real war, then Professor Herman had won the debate hands down. Indeed, if the War on Terror was not a real war, then we as a nation had done an awful lot of illegal stuff, under both the Bush and Obama Administrations. Government agents of the United States of America had involuntarily detained thousands of people without criminal charges and without access to lawyers or judges. We had also killed thousands of people without warning or judicial warrant in a large number of counties around the world to include Sudan, Somalia, Afghanistan, Iraq, Syria, Iran, Pakistan, Yemen, etc. We had also violated our own Constitution by using military commissions to prosecute several individuals at GITMO.

On the other hand, if we were in a state of war, then I won the debate ... hands down. Under the law of war all of the afore listed activities are perfectly legitimate. The ACLU could pontificate from now until Doomsday about how terrible it all was, but they could not say that it was illegal. Not liking something and calling it illegal are two entirely different concepts; there are many things I don't like but they are legal nonetheless. When I wore a younger man's clothes, I recall my elderly torts Alabama law professor telling the class: "It may not always be right, but it is always the law."

To the great dismay of the assembled masses, I methodically proceeded to set out an airtight legal case that the United States of America was in a real war and thus entitled to fully utilize the law of war in the prosecution of said war. I first pointed out that the question of whether or not the War on Terror is a real war can only be answered by looking to the three branches of the U.S. government. Assuredly, in an open society any person is free to voice an opinion as to whether they agree or disagree on this matter, but finality can only be found by objectively examining what the three branches of the government have told us. Under the Constitution, they alone are vested with the authority to speak for the nation. In quick order I demonstrated that all three branches of our government have clearly and unequivocally indicated that the War on Terror is in fact a real war.

From the executive branch: The Constitution vests the power to lead and run the military with the President of the United States. In Article II he is called the Commander in Chief. President Bush believed and acted in a manner consistent with the War on Terror being a real war. President Obama followed suit, although begrudgingly. Both Commanders in Chief kept illegal enemy combatants detained, both killed large numbers of people believed to be illegal enemy combatants, and both employed military commissions at GITMO.

From the Congress: The Congress of the United States never formally "declared war" as empowered in Article I of the Constitution against al-Qa'eda or the Taliban, but there can be no doubt that it "authorized" this War on Terror. In fact, Congress seldom declares war, having done so in only five wars in the nations hundred plus wars. Instead, Congress usually authorizes war by means of a Congressional Resolution to the executive branch. Among the indicators that Congress considers the War on Terror a real war is the 2001 Congressional Authorization for the Use of Military Force (AUMF) against any person, organization, or nation responsible for 9/11.[14] Then there is the striking "war" language first set out in the 2006 Military Commissions Act (passed by the majority Republican Congress) and subsequently followed by the 2009 Military Commissions Act (passed by the majority Democratic Congress).[15]

---

14. Authorization for Use of Military Force (AUMF), Public Law Number 107-40, § 2(a), 115 Stat. 224, 224 (2001) (codified at 50 U.S.C. § 1541).

15. Section 1801 of the Military Commissions Act of 2009 uses the term "unprivileged enemy belligerents" in place of "unlawful enemy combatants." Military Commissions Act of 2009, Pub. L. No. 111-84, § 1801, 123 Stat. 2190, 2574-75 (to be codified at 10 U.S.C. § 948a). Although the

From the Supreme Court: The Supreme Court has rendered opinions in 2004, 2006, and 2008 that are pertinent. All of these generally allow Congress and the President to conduct this conflict under the law of war with some restrictions for those detained at GITMO. In a nutshell, the Court has clearly signaled that the United States has the legal power to designate enemy combatants and detain them until the war is over, subject to additional safeguards, e.g., habeas rights (if detained at GITMO only).[16]

What makes the Supreme Court cases a source of contention is the fact that they are slowly, and quite painfully, developing a new rule of law that will bridge the gap between traditional law of war concepts and domestic criminal law concepts. This is because the enemy is a non-State actor and the law of war was written when nations go to war with other nations. ISIS and al-Qa'eda may be a virtual-State but they are not a nation-State. The greatest consternation with the Court is that given the emerging threat of radical Islam mega-terrorism by means of a WMD, it is unfortunate that the new body of law comes in bits and pieces.

In any event, while it is true that the Supreme Court has signaled some confusion along the way with opinions that are bitterly divided and broadly presented, the judicial phrase that best exemplifies their stamp of approval that we are at war was rendered in 2004 in *Hamdi v. Rumsfeld*,[17] where Justice O'Connor in a plurality opinion (8-1) "made it clear that a *state of war* [which we are still in] is not a blank check for the president [emphasis added] ...."[18]

Needless to say, my presentation upset the ACLU audience with many members voicing emotional dissatisfaction in a vain effort to somehow shame me for daring to speak the truth of the matter. Apparently, it dawned on them that once I had established that all three branches of our government called this a real war, the intellectual

---

language drops "the Taliban" and "associated forces," it specifically lists al-Qa'eda as an unprivileged enemy belligerent. *Id.* at 2575.

16. *Boumediene v. Bush*, 128 S. Ct. 2229 (2008).

17. *See Hamdi v. Rumsfeld*, 542 U.S. 507, 523 (2004) (plurality opinion holding that a U.S. citizen captured in combat operations in Afghanistan could be detained as an enemy combatant).

18. *Id.*

destruction was complete, there was really nothing Professor Herman could say in response.

When it was Herman's turn to take the podium, I could sense that her intended remarks were cast aside as she quickly shifted to a *non sequitur* argument alleging that the United States was detaining the "wrong guy" at GITMO. This is silliness. Even assuming that she was correct and we were detaining an innocent person by mistake that has nothing to do with the legality of the detention facility or the legality of the War on Terror as a general principle of law.

Again, organizations like the ACLU are entitled to their opinions and entitled to voice them as loudly as they wish. The problem is that when they make disingenuous remarks like the "PATRIOT Act is unconstitutional," many Americans immediately take it to heart as a truth and are quickly led astray. The ACLU most certainly knows that they can generally get away with it because their deception is seldom challenged and generally reinforced by liberal commentators in a biased media and educational system. Indeed, there are only a handful of qualified advocates that ever actually stand up to take them on. Anyone can say "we don't like the PATRIOT Act" but nothing is unconstitutional until the Supreme Court says it is unconstitutional.

Chapter 3

Center for Terrorism Law

"War, far as I can see."[1]
—CIA Director Mike Morell

I first started to address the phenomenon of terrorism from an academic perspective just after the attacks of 9/11 when several national news media outlets asked me to opine on the current events developing at home and in Afghanistan. Since that time, I have done over 800 public speeches both in the United States and abroad at universities, public forums, private events, and government institutions. I have testified before both the U.S. Senate and the U.S. House of Representatives as well as lectured on numerous occasions at the Office of Military Commissions, the FBI Academy, the Department of Homeland Security, and all the senior service military academies. Foreign presentations include numerous professional lectures at universities and government institutions in Colombia, Peru, Ukraine, Germany, France, Austria, Canada, Thailand, Japan, India, Honduras, Haiti, Egypt, Kuwait, Panama, Guatemala, Albania, Okinawa, South Korea, England, Mexico, Sweden, Ireland, Scotland, Greece, Israel, Russia, Luxembourg, China,

---

1. Susan Page, *CIA Vet: War "Far As I Can See,"* USA TODAY, May 11, 2015, at A1.

and Uruguay. I have also done over 5,000 appearances on radio, print, and television broadcasts commenting on terrorism issues to include: *Associated Press, New York Times, London Times, Wall Street Journal, Washington Post, Wall Street Journal, USA Today, Miami Herald, Los Angeles Times, Chicago Tribune, Washington Times, Washington Examiner, Army Times, Marine Corps Times, Federal Times, Miami Herald, China Daily*, FOX NEWS, MSNBC, CNN, ABC, PBS, NBC, CBS, NPR, BBC, Voice of Russia, and Al-Jazeera.

Since 2003, most of these activities were conducted in my capacity as the Director of the Center for Terrorism Law. That was the year that St. Mary's University School of Law, located in San Antonio, Texas, created the Center for Terrorism Law. Although I had only been a law professor there for three years, having retired from the Army in 2000, I was appointed as the Director. Texas U.S. Senator John Cornyn provided the keynote remarks to inaugurate the Center and three years later, Texas U.S. Congressman Michael McCall provided the keynote remarks to dedicate the $700,000 facility built to house the new Center (my sister, Deborah E. Addicott graciously provided the funds to build the facility). In 2013, Texas Governor Rick Perry came to San Antonio's renowned La Fogata's Mexican restaurant to deliver opening remarks to celebrate with 300 supporters the 10th Anniversary of the Center for Terrorism Law (former Navy SEAL Marcus Luttrell presented the keynote remarks).

The goal of the Center for Terrorism Law is to examine the current and potential legal issues related to terrorism in the light of achieving and maintaining a proper balance between national security and civil justice. This goal is pursued through research; teaching; professional exchanges such as symposia and consultations; writing, commenting on and publishing written materials; conducting training; and ensuring access to extensive information resources.

The Center also provides assistance free of charge to military personnel wrongfully accused of war crimes and/or Rules of Engagement (ROE) violations while in the performance of combat activities with the forces of radical Islam. We have a very impressive record of success ranging from murder charges dismissed against two Army Green Berets for killing a known enemy combatant in Afghanistan to assisting a Marine junior officer clear his official military record and name for allegedly violating supercilious ROE by shooting a tractor in a combat incident in Afghanistan.[2]

Over the years, the Center for Terrorism Law has emerged as a unique national asset. It continues to function as a 501 (c)(3) charitable entity, operating on private donations from concerned individuals who support its work.

While academic work from the Center for Terrorism Law has seen direct input at Congressional hearings, White House briefings, and Supreme Court arguments, the vast majority of these efforts deal with a variety of technical legal issues associated with terrorism in terms of how civil liberties are weighed in the scales of increased security. In other words, as one would naturally expect to emanate from a law school, the focus at the Center is predominated by issues revolving around legal matters such as detention, intelligence gathering, military commissions, cyber security, targeted killings, law of war, Rules of Engagement, interrogation practices, enforcement compliance, and the like. Far less attention is given to the factors that motivate terrorism even though that is precisely the issue that rubricates the War on Terror. In short, other than to perhaps name it as a label, the analysis of radical Islam receives little attention.

Given our mission statement, the Center's avoidance of in-depth discussions about the religious fuel that motivates radical Islam as the root cause of their terrorism is understandable. Still, this avoidance of the obvious—that radical Islam both condones and commands the many acts of terrorism both here and abroad—has never been lodged as a particular point of criticism towards the Center for Terrorism Law. Until recently, the work at the Center for Terrorism

---

2. See Jeffrey F. Addicott, *The Strange Case of Lieutenant Waddell: How Overly Restrictive Rules of Engagement Adversely Impact the American War Fighter and Undermine Military Victory*, 45 St. Mary's Law Journal 1 (2013).

Law did not run afoul of the sanitized narrative that refuses to provide any credence to the notion that jihadists are what they say they are.

One thing is for certain, radical Islam is spreading not contracting which means that the Center for Terrorism Law will be in operation for many years to come. Even more compelling is the increasing threat of a mass casualty terror attack by means of a WMD. Despite the fact that Americans are not accustomed to long wars, this is now the longest war in American history, and it has only just begun. Europe had its 100 Years War, so will we.[3]

---

3. Marylou Tousignant, *"Europe: 100 Years of War and Transformation"*, THE WASHINGTON POST, August 1, 2014, at A3 *available at* https://www.washingtonpost.com/lifestyle/kidspost/europe-100-years-of-war-and-transformation/2014/07/31/c0116f2a-0b99-11e4-8c9a-923ecc0c7d23_story.html.

Chapter 4

He-Who-Must-Not-Be-Named

"The views of men can only be known, or guessed at, by their words or actions."[1]

—George Washington

The lack of inquisitiveness about radical Islam is not unfamiliar or surprising to most members of the reading public. This wall of silence is everywhere and it has been a constant theme of America's leadership since the beginning of the War on Terror. While the Bush Administration engaged in its own brand of deception regarding the religious-based roots of radical Islam, the Obama Administration went to extraordinary and often Orwellian lengths to avoid any connection of Islam with violence or terrorism at all. The phrase radical Islam was absolutely taboo.

As noted in the Preface, ignoring the overwhelming, incontestable evidence that radical Islam is religious-based is not just the prerogative of our political leadership. This conspiracy of silence is everywhere. Insulated by a coterie of the overly protective, concerned more with running afoul of political correctness than truth telling, the central motif of the War on Terror is largely obscured.

---

1. THE QUOTABLE FOUNDING FATHERS 199 (Buckner F. Melton, Jr. ed., 2004) (statement by George Washington to Patrick Henry, January 15, 1799).

From the mass media, to academia, to all echelons of State and
federal government, radical Islam is often treated in the same manner as the evil protagonist Lord Voldemort in the Harry Potter series—"He-Who-Must-Not-Be-Named."[2]

Radical Islam is the term that must not be uttered and yet it is
an undeniable fact that those who commit the atrocities that continue unabated from every part of the globe do so from a religious
motivation taken directly from a strict constructionist reading of
the primary books considered sacred by those of the Moslem faith.
Commentators may claim that Muslim terrorists try to "invoke
their own deviant, distorted view of Islam in order to justify [terror-
ism],"[3] but the truth is that jihadists unabashedly support their acts
of terror from the orthodoxy of Islam. Muslims like Kareem Abdul-
Jabbar reject these plainly documented Islamic teachings, but they
are in a state of denial when they lament that "[t]hugs, not Muslims,
commit violence in the name of Allah" and that they "pervert the
Quran [Koran] through omission and false interpretation."[4] Again,
Abdul-Jabbar is certainly free to ignore or refuse the specific teachings of Islam that validate the terror of jihad, but he cannot ignore
the fact that these Muslim doctrines do not rely on historically false
or tortured interpretations. Rejecting them is preferable, of course,
but pretending that they do not exist or wishing them away is disingenuous and dangerous.

Nevertheless, Abdul-Jabbar's approach that radical Islam is not
Islamic sums up the longstanding United States policy, for both
Barack Hussein Obama and his predecessor, George W. Bush. This
disinformation campaign to deny the existence of radical Islam was
repeatedly stated by both administrations since 9/11.

Both President Obama and President Bush consistently refrained
from referring to groups such as al-Qa'eda and ISIS as "radical Islamists" and instead employed generic blanket descriptions such as
"lone-wolfs," "terrorists," "extremists," or "evildoers." Countries

---

2.   J.K. Rowling, HARRY POTTER AND THE SORCERER'S STONE (1997).
3.   *See* Eli Lake, *Why Obama Can't Say Radical Islam*, BLOOMBERG, January
19, 2015.
4.   Kareem Abdul-Jabbar, *Paris Was Not About Religion*, TIME, January 26,
2015, at 29.

all over the world, to include Muslim-majority nations like Egypt and Jordan, openly recognize that the enemy is radical Islam and understand the fact that most Muslims do not practice violent jihad, but the leaders of our country refuse to make that distinction. In turn, without proper leadership, America's low information voters follow the pied piper of Hamelin to their detriment.

One has to search long and hard for something along the lines of the March 2009 cover of *Newsweek* magazine where radical Islam was frankly described by Muslim writer Fareed Zakaria (Zakaria's father was a Muslim scholar in India), as a "fact of life."[5] Despite the fact that millions of Muslims are infected by the virus of radical Islam and that "radical Islam has gained a powerful foothold"[6] both "in the Muslim imagination"[7] and in repeated expressions of overt violence, honest and informed discussion is squelched.

The truth of the matter is that vast numbers of Muslims claim legal and moral justification for murder and other vicious crimes against humanity because they take a strict view of bedrock principles found in the religion of Islam. In short they believe to the death that Islam itself commands them to commit these vile acts of terror. They believe they possess the monopoly on the true Islam. As Osama bin Laden put it in a video clip released just after 9/11: "The attacks made people think about ... *true* Islam, which benefited them greatly."[8]

The Bush Administration & Radical Islam

President Bush's position on the nature of the enemy was first revealed in remarks he gave at the Islamic Center of Washington D.C. just days after the 9/11 attacks:

---

5. Fareed Zakaria, *Learning to Live with Radical Islam*, NEWSWEEK, March 9, 2009, at 25.

6. *Id.* at 28.

7. *Id.*

8. *See* James M. Dorsey, *Some Fear Bin Laden Video Will Strain Relations Between U.S. and Saudi Arabia*, WALL STREET JOURNAL, December 17, 2001, at A13.

The face of terror is not the true faith of Islam. That's not what Islam is all about. Islam is peace. These terrorists don't represent peace, they represent evil and war.[9]

Bush has never elaborated on his assertion that "Islam is [a religion of] peace." He certainly could not be referencing the manner in which Islam initially spread its empire. As a student of history, it is impossible to accurately describe the early spread of the religion of Islam as some sort of a peaceful "civil rights" movement. In those formative years, and for many years to follow, Islam spread by fire and sword. Furthermore, Bush's idea that the religion of Islam has little to do with the people that conducted the attacks on 9/11 is equally spurious. They were all Muslims and attacked America in the name of the religion of Islam, albeit radical Islam.

Bush's closest brush with truth telling occurred in his address to a joint session of the U.S. Congress on September 20, 2001:

The terrorists who attacked the United States practice a fringe form of Islamic extremism that has been rejected by Muslim scholars and the vast majority of Muslim clerics … a fringe movement that perverts the peaceful teachings of Islam .... The terrorists are traitors to their own faith, trying, in effect, to hijack Islam itself. The enemy of America is not our many Muslim friends; it is not our many Arab friends. Our enemy is a radical network of terrorists, and every government that supports them.[10]

In the main, Bush's subsequent public statements on radical Islam followed the theme that there is no real connection between the Muslim terrorists and the religion of Islam. One news outlet recently cataloged the statements of Bush and Obama.[11] For example:

---

9. *See* White House Archives (9/17/2001).
10. George W. Bush, Address to the Nation – September 20, 2001.
11. *See* Eli Lake, *Why Obama Can't Say Radical Islam*, BLOOMBERG, January 19, 2015.

"Ours is a war not against a religion, not against the Muslim faith. But ours is a war against individuals who absolutely hate what America stands for."—Bush

"Our enemy doesn't follow the great traditions of Islam. They've hijacked a great religion."—Bush

"There are thousands of Muslims who proudly call themselves Americans, and they know what I know – that the Muslim faith is based upon peace and love and compassion."—Bush

"Our war is not against Islam, or against faith practiced by the Muslim people. Our war is a war against evil."—Bush

Whether President Bush actually believed that Islamic religious dogma had nothing to do with jihadist terror attacks or not, Elliot Abrams, who served as a Deputy National Security adviser, defended the Bush Administration's soft-shoe approach saying:

We were invading two Muslim countries, and we were being accused of being at war with Islam. So, the administration wanted to make it very clear that we are not at war with Islam and every Muslim in the world.[12]

Again, it is certain that not all Muslims support the concept of violent jihad as a means to spread Islam, but millions do.[13] What made Bush's statements so unsettling was that he never seemed to comprehend that it is better to state the truth about the nature of radical Islam rather than self-censor speech so as not to offend. The starting point in defeating any enemy requires that the enemy

---

12. *Id.*
13. *See generally* Jacob Poushter, *Extremism Concerns Growing in West and Predominantly Muslim Countries*, PEW RESEARCH CENTER, July 16, 2015.

should be regarded and evaluated in the light of reality and not the intellectual corruption that emanates from political expediency. A Statesman does not tell people what they might want to hear, that is the realm of the politician. The Statesman calls it what it is. Unfortunately, rarely do politics and leadership converge to produce a Statesman.

The Obama Administration & Radical Islam

One misconception frequently repeated and often challenged in dealing with radical Islamic terrorism is that it is not important to dwell on the characteristics or motivations of the person or persons conducting a particular terror attack—they are simply terrorists, or in many cases, if Obamaism thinking is used, it is not terrorism at all. It is workplace violence.

That the Obama Administration refused to link terror attacks in the United States to Islam is well known. Not only did President Obama downplay any mention of radical Islam as the chief motivator for our enemies, he consistently tried to dismiss the very idea that we are even in a War on Terror.

President Obama's expressed desire to dismantle key elements of the Bush policies *vis-à-vis* al-Qa'eda, the Taliban, and associated forces began only days after taking the oath of office in 2009. Instead of creating an interagency task force to conduct a detailed study of all viable options and recommendations on how best to proceed in the War on Terror, the President issued executive orders mandating what were billed as sweeping changes in policy. In three executive orders issued on January 22, 2009, the President ordered: (1) the closure of Guantanamo Bay within one year;[14] (2) the suspension of all ongoing military commissions;[15] and (3) the suspension of the CIA's enhanced interrogation program.[16] Ironically, within one year of the announcement, two of the executive orders would be, for all practical purposes, functionally nullified.

---

14. Exec. Order No. 13,492, 74 Fed. Reg. 4897, 4898 (Jan. 22, 2009); *see also* Exec. Order No. 13,493, 74 Fed. Reg. 4901 (Jan. 22, 2009) (establishing a special task force on detainee disposition).
15. Exec. Order No. 13,492, 72 Fed. Reg. at 4899 (Jan 22, 2009).
16. Exec. Order No. 13,491, 74 Fed. Reg. 4893, 4894 (Jan. 22, 2009).

After eight years of his presidency, GITMO is still open and military commissions still function (albeit slowly). In addition, in case anyone was noticing, Obama's indignation about the "Bush" CIA interrogation techniques was pure nonsense, the program stopped under the Bush Administration in 2004.

In fact, during his entire time in office, President Obama made only one unequivocal statement that America was at "[W]ar against al-Qa'eda."[17] Paradoxically, this statement was made only after the intense criticism of Obama for treating al-Qa'eda operative Umar Farouk Abdulmutallab, who was dispatched from Yemen by al-Qa'eda to detonate an explosive device on a U.S. aircraft flying over Detroit on Christmas Day 2009, as a common criminal with Miranda rights.

The end result of Obama's eight long years of obfuscation is that most Americans are left utterly confused about the meaning of the War on Terror. For example, the *New York Times* editorial page of October 4, 2011, carried six letters to the editor on the topic of the drone strike that killed al-Qa'eda chief Anwar al-Awlaki, an American citizen in Yemen.[18] Of those six letters, only one of them understood that the killing was an entirely lawful act carried out under the law of war. All the others reflected varying degrees of confusion that included sentiments that the United States was: (1) wrong for not operating under domestic criminal law to arrest al-Awlaki; (2) wrong for killing a U.S. citizen; or (3) that the rule of law didn't really matter because al-Awlaki was a "bad guy" and "we have to do what we have to do (the law of the jungle)."

Amazingly, not a single voice in the Obama Administration took the time to defend the action as lawful under a simple set of legal parameters related to the law of war. Instead, the White House

---

17. President Barack Obama, Remarks by the President on Strengthening Intelligence and Aviation Security, (Jan. 7, 2010) *available at* 2010 WL 40113 ("We are at war. We are at war against al Qaeda, a far-reaching network of violence and hatred that attacked us on 9/11, that killed nearly 3,000 innocent people, and that is plotting to strike us again. And we will do whatever it takes to defeat them.").

18. Letters to the Editor, *The Killing of a Qaeda Leader in Yemen*, New York Times, October 4, 2011, at A22.

issued statements associated with the fact that we were "defending" ourselves against a terrorist, even though the foundational rule of law justification has nothing to do with the fact that al-Awlaki was a "terrorist" or a bad person. The justification for America's lawful use of force against al-Awlaki was as follows: (1) the United States is at war with al-Qaeda; (2) the law of war rule of law applies to this war, not the domestic criminal law rule of law; (3) the law of war allows the United States to kill on sight any unlawful enemy combatant (to include a U.S. citizen al-Qa'eda member), detain indefinitely any unlawful enemy combatant, or use military commissions when appropriate (unless the nation imposes self-restrictions).

Of course, Obama generally preferred to avoid the use of the word terror at all if he could because he knew full well that the term terror is immediately associated not with right or left-wing extremist groups but with radical Muslims. Still, in the hierarchy of disinformation, the word terror is better than the word Islamist.

Below is a sampling of some of President Obama's remarks on Muslim terror. Throughout his presidency, President Obama not only mirrored President Bush in his obfuscation of radical Islam, he vastly exceeded it.[19]

"They're terrorists. And we are not at war with Islam. We are at war with people who have perverted Islam."— Obama

"The terrorists do not speak for over a billion Muslims who reject their hateful ideology."— Obama

"How do we, as people of faith, reconcile these realities – the profound good ... the compassion and love that can flow from all of our faiths, operating alongside those who seek to hijack religion for their own murderous ends?"— Obama.

19. Eli Lake, *Why Obama Can't Say Radical Islam*, Bloomberg, January 19, 2015.

"This great religion in the hands of a few extremists has been distorted to justify violence." — Obama.

With the Paris attacks in 2015, Obama coined the term "violent extremism" in hopes that he could cover up Islamic driven murder as simply just one type of terrorism amongst many types of terrorism. But the truth is that Islamic terror attacks dramatically increased under President Obama's watch — both in the United States and across the globe. Radical Islam obviously did not get the Obama memo (or CD of selected Obama speeches) of "hope and change."[20]

President Bush could rightly claim that no attacks by radical Islam occurred on his two-term watch after 9/11, Obama could not. In fact, Obama's first year in office saw two attacks on the homeland by radical jihadists. One in Arkansas by a convert to Islam named Abdulhakim Mujahid Muhammad who used a semi-automatic rifle to shoot to death one military soldier (Private William Long) and wound another at an Army recruiting station. The other terror attack was conducted by Nidal Malik Hasan who shot and killed 13 soldiers and wounded scores more at Fort Hood, Texas.[21]

Although both terror attacks were clearly motivated by radical Islam and therefore should have been tried in federal court, which has primary jurisdiction for all terror cases, Obama immediately deemed the terror attack in Arkansas as a random criminal act and refused to assert federal authority to prosecute. After all, under Obama rationale, radical Islamic terror can no longer happen in America so it has to be ignored or repackaged. Instead, Obama's Justice Department turned the case over to the State of Arkansas where Muhammad was prosecuted under State law for murder and sentenced to life.

Under the same Obama mantra of denial, the 2009 jihadi terror attack at Fort Hood, Texas, was deemed to be a case of workplace

20. Two of Obama's campaign slogans were: "Hope and Change" and "Change We Can Believe In," see Presidential Campaign Slogans, http://www.presidentsusa.net/campaignslogans.html.
21. Nancy Gibb, Terrified . . . Or Terrorist?, TIME, November 23, 2009, at 26.

violence and primary federal jurisdiction was again declined. Hasan was tried in a military court for murder and sentenced to death. Still, taking marching orders from the Obama Administration, no charges of terrorism were brought up by the military, despite Hasan's proud claim that he was fighting with his fellow *mujahedeen* (one who is engaged in jihad) brothers as a warrior for Allah. While these two instances perfectly describe the attitude of the Obama Administration when it came to identifying the *modus vivendi* of radical Islam, as we have already seen, the Bush Administration was not without fault; similar views predominated.

Obama's senior counter-terrorism adviser, John Brennan, proclaimed Obama's policy of denial of radical Islam in 2010. Through *bias by story selection* (taking a selected view, but ignoring the main view) and *bias by selection of sources* (choosing an "expert" you agree with) Brennan even tried to redefine basic Islamic terminology:

> The President's strategy is absolutely clear about the threat we face .... Nor do we describe our enemy as "jihadists" or "Islamists" because jihad is a holy struggle, a legitimate tenet of Islam, meaning to purify oneself or one's community, and there is nothing holy or legitimate or Islamic about murdering innocent men, women and children .... Moreover, describing our enemy in religious terms would lend credence to the lie – propagated by al Qaeda and its affiliates to justify terrorism – that the United States is somehow at war against Islam.[22]

Not only did the Obama Administration reflect an oblivious attitude about radical Islam,[23] there was always a definite aloofness and dismissiveness in the President's tone about the threat of radical Islam. It is almost as if the whole matter was beneath him and not worthy of his time or effort. This attitude permeated the Obama

---

22. See "Remarks by Assistant to the President for Homeland Security and Counterterrorism John Brennan at CSIS." *The White House*, 26 May 2010.
23. Eli Lake, *Why Obama Can't Say Radical Islam*, BLOOMBERG, January 19, 2015.

Administration to the point that it often appeared to be a theater of the absurd. Any and every excuse was provided to avoid the truth that radical Islam is fueled and fostered by a religious orthodoxy.

Responding to complaints that the Obama Administration would not identify radical Islam, U.S. Department of State deputy spokeswoman, Marie Harf, perfectly exemplified this attitude of denial. Harf stated that the real problem with "He-Who-Must-Not-Be-Named," was not a religious matter at all, it was simply that "they" had no jobs:

> We cannot win this war by killing them …. We need … in the medium and longer-term to go after the root causes that lead people to join these groups, whether it's lack of opportunity for jobs ….[24]

Perhaps the most preposterous attempt at radical Islam avoidance came with Obama's response to the January 2015 jihadi terror attack on *Charlie Hebdo* in Paris. Obama did not attend, or even send a high-level American official to, the million-person rally in Paris led by over 40 world leaders to identify and denounce radical Islam. Why? Because the "great and powerful Oz has spoken," radical Islam must not be named, no matter the facts.

In this vein, White House press secretary Joshua Earnest stated: "We have chosen not to use that label [radical Islam] because it does not seem to accurately describe what happened in Paris."[25] In double talk that bordered on the surreal, Earnest continued with a straight face and stated that of greatest concern to the Obama White House was "accuracy."

> We want to describe exactly what happened. These are individuals who carried out an act of terrorism, and they *later* tried to justify that act of terrorism by invoking the reli-

---

24. Selwin Duke, *Obama Anti-Terrorism Jobs for Jihadists is a Marxist Idea*, THE NEW AMERICAN, February 19, 2015.
25. Press briefing by Press Secretary Josh Earnest on January 15, 2015. Full transcript *available at*: https://www.whitehouse.gov/the-press-office/2015/01/12/press-briefing-press-secretary-josh-earnest-1122015.

gion of Islam and their own deviant view of it" [emphasis added].[26]

Wait, what? Think about it. Obama's official spokesman is stating that on January 7, 2015, the *Charlie Hebdo* attackers carrying Kalashnikov assault rifles, rocket propelled grenades, and submachine guns, just randomly targeted 12 victims at the Paris newspaper office that had just happened to make fun of Muhammad with some cartoons, and then only *after* they committed the murders did they realize that they had no justification for their actions so they just chalked it up to their Islamic faith. Even my 7th grader could see through this absurdity of twisted thinking.

One has to really wonder if anyone at the White House even watched the cell phone video showing the real time actions of the two heavily armed men during the shooting spree. They are seen clad in their jihadi black uniforms and hooded with distinctive black masks, repeatedly screaming in the streets of Paris: "*Allah-u-akbar*" (God is greater), "*Allah-u-akbar*" (God is greater), and "We have avenged the Prophet Muhammed?"[27]

What then did Obama do? In his familiar pattern of appearing to do something when in fact doing nothing, Obama reacted to the criticism regarding his non-response by holding one of his never ending White House summits. This one was entitled: "Violent Extremism." Not only was the FBI, the lead federal agency charged with investigating terrorism in the United States, not invited to the White House summit, but nothing in the title suggested anything about radical Islam, the number one threat to the nation and the world in terms of violent extremism. This was too much, even for the left leaning media.

On January 12, 2015, Earnest was pelted with questions at a White House press conference about whether the recent acts of Islamic extremism would be discussed at the upcoming summit. The following is an excerpt of the absolutely half-witted answers given by Obama's official spokesman:

---

26. *See id.*
27. Dan Bilefsky and Maia De La Baume, *Terrorists Strike Charlie Hebdo Newspaper in Paris*, NEW YORK TIMES, January 17, 2015, at A1.

<u>Reporter Question</u>: And will you speak about the battle against Islamist extremism [at the summit on violent extremism]?

<u>Mr. Earnest</u>: Well, all forms of violent extremism would certainly be discussed in the context of this summit. But obviously the threat that we see from violent extremism in which individuals invoke the name of Islam, an otherwise peaceful religion, as they carry out these attacks would certainly be obviously a priority in the discussion here.

<u>Reporter Question</u>: Josh, why wouldn't you use the phrase right there, that we are going to take on Islamist extremism? You said all forms of violent extremism.

<u>Mr. Earnest</u>: She [the previous reporter] asked me what the summit would discuss, and all forms of violent extremism would be discussed, and obviously the most potent and certainly the most graphic display that we've seen in recent days is, again, motivated by those individuals that seek to invoke the name of Islam to carry out these violent attacks. And that's certainly something that we want to work very hard to counter and mitigate, and we've got a strategy that we've been discussing for some time to exactly do that.

<u>Reporter Question</u>: So if it's the most potent form, according to you, of extremism, why isn't the summit on countering Islamic extremism?

<u>Mr. Earnest</u>: Because violent extremism is something that we want to be focused on, and it's not just Islamic violent extremism that we want to counter; there are other forms of

. . . .

<u>Reporter Question</u>: The recent cases in Paris, Australia, Canada - isn't the thread through them that it's Islamic extremism?

<u>Mr. Earnest</u>: Well, certainly the examples that you cite are examples of individuals who have cited Islam as they've carried out acts of violence. There's no arguing that.[28]

---

28. Press briefing by Press Secretary Josh Earnest on January 12, 2015, https://www.whitehouse.gov/the-press-office/2015/01/12/press-briefing-press-secretary-josh-earnest-1122015.

The Obama White House also refrained from identifying the favored victims of radical Islam—Jews and Christians. For example, it characterized the Jewish victims murdered by the ISIS inspired jihadist at the Paris kosher market (this separate attack took place during the time frame of the attacks on *Charlie Hebdo*) as "random," i.e., not targeted because they were Jewish. Then in February 2015, Earnest referred to the ISIS beheading of 21 Coptic Christians on a beach in Libya, as simply "Egyptian citizens" and never bothered to mention their Christian faith which was exactly why their red blood was poured out on the white sand of that beach.[29] Jews and Christians are targeted by radical Islam because of their faith.

When it came to dealing with ISIS, Obama generally employed the same strategy of denying any connection of radical Islam with Islam. A typical Obama observation:

> Now let's make two things clear: ISIL [ISIS] is not 'Islamic.' No religion condones the killing of innocents, and the vast majority of ISIL's [ISIS's] victims have been Muslim .... ISIL [ISIS] is a terrorist organization, pure and simple. And it has no vision other than the slaughter of all who stand in its way."[30]

However, at America's National Prayer Breakfast on February 5, 2015, Obama did shift gears and tried a new tactic of distortion. Instead of the usual head in the sand denial approach, Obama employed a sort of moral equivalency argument, pointing to the historical fact that Christians in the past had committed murder as well.

> We see ISIL [ISIS], a brutal, vicious death cult that, in the name of religion, carries out unspeakable acts of barba-

---

29. Clyne, Melissa, *Hayden: Obama Trapped by Own Words on Islamic Terror*, Newsmax, February 17, 2015, http://www.newsmax.com/Headline/Michael-Hayden-Obama-radical-Islam-terror/2015/02/17/id/625203/
30. *See* Transcript: President Obama's Speech on Combating ISIS - CNNPolitics.com.

rism—terrorizing religious minorities like the Yezidis, sub-
jecting women to rape as a weapon of war, and claiming the
mantle of religious authority for such actions .... And lest
we get on our high horse and think this is unique to some
other place, remember that during the Crusades and the Inquisition, people committed terrible deeds in the name of
Christ.[31]

While Obama's observations are true, they are at best sopho-
moric and not pertinent to the here and now. The Inquisition was
500 years ago and during the Crusades, a thousand years ago, both
Muslim and Christian forces committed equivalent atrocities. Apart
from the fact that radical Muslims can point to their holy texts to
justify their murders—both then and now—and Christians cannot
(see Chapter 11), we are living in the present. Today's murderers
are Muslims killing in the name of Islam, not Christians killing in
the name of Christ.

As with President Bush, why did President Obama consistently
refuse to acknowledge the truth about radical Islam and ISIS? ISIS
is Islamic, ISIS is religious, and ISIS most certainly does have a
vision—the conquest of the world for Allah. Perhaps President
Obama believed that by playing down the threat of radical Islam,
it would go away on its own. Perhaps it was a function of his formative years spent in Muslim schools in Indonesia. Or perhaps, as
one commentator speculated, Obama wants the American people to
"maintain a proper perspective and not provide a victory to these
terrorist networks by overinflating their importance—and suggesting, in some fashion, that they are an existential threat to the United
States or the world order."[32]

But things are changing with the American people. With the rise
of the ISIS, many Americans are no longer satisfied with the narrative that we must tip toe around the issue of the religious nature of

31. *Obama Condemns Those Who 'Hijack Religion,'* USA Today, February
6, 2015, 5A.
32. Fareed Zakaria, *Learning to Live with Radical Islam,* Newsweek, March 9,
2009, at 25.

radical Islam. Even MSNBC's liberal-leaning talk show, *Morning Joe,* voiced frustration and alarm about the Obama Administration's refusal to identify the nature of the enemy. In a segment broadcast February 17, 2015, the co-host, Joe Scarborough, said:

> Generals always say you got to know the enemy, who is the enemy, who are you fighting against, who does this, why are they doing this ... [we know the terrorists] don't do this because they're a bunch of sociopaths, they do this because they are radical Islamists at the rawest most base form . . . and they are seeking to provoke the world into Armageddon, they believe they are Allah's agent for end times . . . [we can't] continue like we are having a humanities class or a seminar on radical Islam .... We need to know the enemy, call out the enemy, and call it what it is, radical Islam.[33]

Similarly, the liberal-leaning *New York Times* complained about President Obama's leadership approach of using phrases like "dark ideology" instead of radical Islam, when "tens of millions of Muslims" fit that very description:

> To call this movement, whose most potent recent manifestation is the Islamic State, a 'dark ideology' is like calling Nazism a reaction to German humiliation in World War I: true but wholly inadequate. There is little point in Western politicians rehearsing lines about there being no battle between Islam and the West, when in all the above-mentioned countries tens of millions of Muslims, with much carnage as evidence, believe the contrary.[34]

---

33. Scarborough, Joe, *'Americans Are Frustrated' Obama Won't Call Radical Islam What It Is,* Real Clear Politics, February 17, 2015, http://www.realclearpolitics.com/video/2015/02/17/joe_scarborough_americans_are_frustrated_obama_wont_call_radical_islam_what_it_is.html.
34. Cohen, Roger, *Islam and the West at War,* New York Times, February 16, 2015, at A1. http://www.nytimes.com/2015/02/17/opinion/roger-cohen-islam-and-the-west-at-war.html?_r=0.

The United States is the most powerful nation in the world and a prime target for the machinations of radical Islam. If not in the name of moral clarity, then in the name of strategic clarity, American leadership must identify the preeminent source of terror as radical Islam. If an American president would have the courage to do so, the American people "as well as the vast majority of Muslims around the world, would be well pleased that the most powerful government in the world is finally speaking the truth about the people who are threatening us and civilized people everywhere and is going on the ideological offensive against them."[35]

Some of the strongest critics of Obama's policy regarding radical Islam and ISIS came from senior members who served in the second term of the Obama Administration. Leon Panetta, the former director of the Central Intelligence Agency (CIA), charged the rise of ISIS directly to President Obama's decision to pull out of Iraq too quickly while failing to respond fast enough to the civil war in Syria.[36] Panetta commented on CBS's *60 Minutes*, that Obama's entire national security team urged him to provide more support to the non-radical Islamic fighters seeking to overthrow Syria's Assad. Obama refused. In turn, Secretary of Defense Robert Gates wrote in his book after leaving office, that Obama never viewed the wars of Iraq and Afghanistan as inherited and that the Obama policy was to just get out no matter what.[37]

It was not only Americans who took notice of Obama's weak stance when it came to national security, even our enemies mocked us. For instance, Ali Youseni, a senior advisor to Iranian President Hassan Rouhani, called Obama the weakest U.S. president in American history with a leadership style that was humiliating.[38]

---

35. Herf, Jeffrey, *Time for a Reset*, New Republic, February 5, 2011.

36. Howell, Kellan, *Former Obama Secretaries Panetta, Gates Criticize President on Islamic State Handling*, Washington Times, September 20, 2014, at A1.

37. Bob Woodward, *Robert Gates, Former Defense Secretary, Offers Harsh Critique of Obama's Leadership in "Duty,"* Washington Post, January 7, 2014, at A1.

38. Sandy Fitzgerald, *Top Iranian Adviser: Obama Is "Weakest of US Presidents,"* Newsmax, April 21, 2014.

Yet, President Obama persisted to the end of his term with the incorrect assessment that, because radical Muslims' actions and beliefs do not align with peaceful Muslims' actions and beliefs, radical Muslims could not possibly be acting pursuant to Islam. At the end of the day, it matters little whether radical Muslims "properly understand" the dictates of Islam as others may define them; rather, it matters that they believe to the death that they are acting for Allah in their jihadi quest to ultimately reach a 72-virgin paradise as the heavenly reward for the *shahid* (martyr).[39]

39. *See generally,* Abu Hurairah, The Book on Virtues of Jihad, Jami at-Tirmidhi – Sunna; J. MacDonald, *Islamic Eschatology VI-Paradise,* Islamic Studies, 5, 352-360 (1966).

Chapter 5

God and Religion

"What is the truth?"[1]

—Pontius Pilate

There are three primary factors that hinder an open discussion of radical Islam and they are all fear-based. They are: (1) the general avoidance fear of speaking about religion; (2) the fear of physical harm to self; and (3) the fear of the viciousness of political correctness.

The solution to fear is courage. If the realization that life is just too short to live in the shadow of fear does not provide the proper impetus to press forward, then the truism that the "more things you fear, the more you *will* fear" should ring loud and clear. To paraphrase Shakespeare, "a coward dies a thousand times, but a brave man only once."[2] The solution to those cow-towed by a mental attitude of fear, is to stand for freedom of thought. Challenge the status quo when it is absurd; ignore the voices of the herd and employ in-

---

1. *John* 18:38. ("Pilate saith unto him [Jesus], What is truth? And when he had said this, he went out again to the Jews, and saith unto them, I find no fault at all."). Pontius Pilate was the Roman Procurator of Judea, AD 26–36. Although Pilate found Jesus of Nazareth not guilty under Roman law, he sentenced him to death by Roman crucifixion.
2. William Shakespeare, JULIUS CAESAR (1684).

dependent thinking. Never be content to live your life in Thoreau's "quiet desperation."[3]

This chapter is about religion and we shall, of necessity, fearlessly venture into the deep waters. Because radical Islam is motivated by religion, it is necessary to explore the matter of religion in general and then later in specific terms.

The premise that people are extremely uncomfortable when their religious beliefs are questioned or scrutinized is most certainly correct, but it nonetheless seems rather curious on its face. If a particular set of religious beliefs are considered valuable and valid then why should they be a source of embarrassment or non-discussion? To put it another way, if someone believes in a particular concept concerning God, it would seem natural that they would be more than happy to engage anyone in a discussion of those beliefs as long as the forum was civil in nature and tone.

War & Religion

When Karl Marx wrote that religion is the "opium of the people,"[4] he was referring to the fact that religion has long been used by those in power to control the social, political, and cultural behavior of the masses, with little or no concern for the content or validity of the underlying theological principles. Indeed, there is no question that the psychological forces associated with religion have played a powerful role in controlling and channeling human behavior across a broad spectrum, even to the point where monstrous horrors have been committed in the name of God. People of all religions are guilty. To be sure, however, this does not necessarily mean that the religion itself is at fault; only that the people that have used, or misused, the religion are at fault.

As even the novice student of history knows, the relationship between religion and war has existed for a very long time. A brief

3. Henry David Thoreau, *Civil Disobedience and Other Essays* (1993).
4. Karl Marx, Contribution to the Critique of Hegel's Philosophy of Right, *in* THE PORTABLE KARL MARX 115 (Eugene Kamenka ed., Penguin 1983) (1843) (one of Karl Marx's most often quoted phrases, found in the introduction of his work and translated from the German *"Die Religion . . . ist das Opium des Volkes"*).

review of human history reveals that various individuals, groups, and nations have used religion as a pretext to engage in aggression against others. While the purely seated religious wars in the West ceased with the end of the Thirty Years War (1618–1648), a horrible affair where the Catholics and Protestants of Europe were slaughtering each other, religion still plays a role in shaping history.

For instance, reflecting the idea that God was on their side, the Nazis in World War II issued a metallic military belt buckle to their infantry that was stamped with the phrase: *Gott Mit Uns* (God With Us).[5] In turn, it is no surprise that the Islamic radicalism that fuels the War on Terror employs the Muslim religion in order to cloak a lust for domination through despicable expressions of unlawful violence, primarily targeting innocent civilians (Muslims, Christians, and Jews).

On the other hand, when it comes to confronting the forces of radical Islam, it is not surprising that democracies like the United States of America will also employ religious symbolism to support the necessary use of force in self-defense. Despite the fact that all American presidents, including Barack Obama, have invoked religious themes in time of war, the use of religion in this context is generally subordinate to the more predominant and commonsense themes of self-defense and national patriotism. Even if our enemies disingenuously assert that they also are acting in self-defense, the right to defend oneself from aggressive violence is inviolable.

Truth-Seekers

Like many words, the term religion is subject to a variety of meanings. According to the American Heritage College Dictionary, the most ordinary definition would mean "[b]elief in and reverence for a supernatural power or powers regarded as creator and governor of the universe," but it also means, "[a] set of beliefs, values, and

---

5. *See* Adolf Hitler, MEIN KAMPF 65 (Ralph Mannheim ed., 1999) (1925) ("Hence today I believe that I am acting in accordance with the will of the Almighty Creator: by defending myself against the Jew, I am fighting for the work of the Lord.").

practices based on the teachings of a spiritual leader."[6] Interesting-ly, a generalized comparative study of the world's major religions reveals that one can easily subdivide them into two specific and distinct categories: *works-religion* and *grace-religion*.

Each day, around the world, there are those who begin and end their day by turning to the sacred writings of their religious tradi-tions for comfort and guidance, understanding, and enlightenment. In the brief sojourn of mankind, seven major world religions have arisen and set out their beliefs in writing. These works are Hindu-ism's *Bhagavad Gita*, Judaism's *Tanakh*, Confucianism's *Analects*, Taoism's *Tao Te Ching*, Buddhism's *Dhammapada*, Christianity's *Bible (Old and New Testament)*, and Islam's *Koran*.

Religious books are not texts for the study of life sciences, but rather books that claim to be about God and His plan and purpose for mankind. In this regard, Hindus, Jews, Confucians, Taoists, Buddhists, Christians, and Muslims each claim that their book best reveals God(s) and offers the better or, in some cases, the only an-swer to the meaning of life. Such being the case, critics ask how it is possible to know which religion, if any, is correct. This, of course, sums up the real intellectual challenge associated with religion and raises the most profound question one can ask: What is [the] truth? Pontius Pilate, the Roman governor of Judea asked this very ques-tion in AD 30, but only in a rhetorical sense.

Surprisingly, a predominating factor one encounters in posing questions about the truth revolves around the astonishing amount of apathy; most people simply have no desire to challenge themselves to even frame the question: Which religion is the truth? Content to incorporate as their own whatever religious belief system they were born into—no matter how illogical or ill-conceived—independent thinking and reasoning have little, if anything, to do with how the mass of humanity comes to personalize a religious belief. For in-stance, you are a Hindu for no other reason except that your parents were Hindu. Or, you are a Muslim because your parents were Mus-lim.

---

6. AMERICAN HERITAGE COLLEGE DICTIONARY 1153 (3rd ed. 1997).

Still, people have free will, and in each generation there are those who find this follow-the-leader approach to religion wholly unsatisfactory. These are what I call the *truth-seekers*. Men and women who base their personal religious beliefs not on the happenstance of their cultural birthright or other environmental factors (such as religious conversion due to a marriage partner of a different faith), but on a foundation which evaluates the full range of religious options and then makes an informed decision.

Clearly, for someone who insists a concern for truth, there is absolutely no subject more important to which the human mind can address itself. In the context of religion, one item is abundantly certain. We are all riding a death train and one day it will make a stop and each of us will have to get off. Furthermore, there is no U-Haul following the hearse to the gravesite (you can't take your worldly possessions with you).

Now given that there are seven major religions, the odds that you are born into the correct religion is one in seven, not good odds at Vegas, providing any of the seven are accurate. Still, unlike the infamous Pontius Pilate who disingenuously asked, "What is [the] truth?" and then refused to intellectually consider the answer, the truth-seeker is not discouraged by the fact that various world religions are in competition for the ultimate truth. Of necessity, truth should encourage honest scrutiny. The true religion is intrinsic, and given a level intellectual playing field, it will always prevail for the truth-seeker.

So what can be said about the origin of religion? As long as humans have looked out into the night sky, it seems apparent that some have set aside the obvious social and cultural forces associated with religion and given a great deal of careful thought about what constitutes the real nature of God. Anyone, even the agnostic, can rationally conclude that God exists, but no human can discern the nature of God—who He is.[7] Therefore, if one accepts the premise

---

7. For an excellent discussion of this *see* Jeffrey F. Addicott, *Storm Clouds on the Horizon of Darwinism: Teaching the Anthropic Principle and Intelligent Design in the Public Schools*, 63 Ohio State Law Journal 1508 (2002).

that God exists, it is entirely reasonable to assume two points. First, God makes sense. And second, He purposefully reveals Himself in a sensible fashion, in the language and culture of the particular time frame in which any human resides, to those individuals who desire to know Him. As one brilliant theologian once stated, God does not "hide the ball" to the truth seeker.[8]

Unfortunately, from a historical perspective, much of this God-directed activity toward people is difficult to chronicle, as the vast majority of the human experience in this field has been based on oral traditions, leaving few traces of record. We can only say with certainty that archeological evidence associated with some of the earliest human grave sites unequivocally demonstrate that people have always held some kind of belief in an afterlife. Meaningful information about God's revelations can only be found in the historic period of man's sojourn when writing was developed. This era did not begin until, at most, a mere 5,000 years ago in the Tigris-Euphrates River valley. Since that time, seven major religions have emerged, each leaving written records to stand for consideration, Islam being the last.

Commonalities of Religion
Anyone who has taken the time to engage in the study of comparative religion realizes that it is virtually impossible to catalogue all the many variations and sub-groupings that reside in each of them. Nevertheless, certain broad generalities can easily be drawn. Thus, apart from all the things that can be said about Hinduism, Buddhism, Confucianism, Taoism, Islam, Judaism, or Christianity, when one boils each of them down to their bottom lines—to their basic beliefs—there emerge four central themes that are shared as base commonalities:

> (1) All religions agree that the nature of man either is or becomes tainted with sin. Man is a morally flawed creature relative to God(s). In other words, man is imperfect and God is perfect. Man is unrighteous and God is righteous.

8.   *See* R. B. Thieme, Jr., THE PLAN OF GOD 4 (2014).

    (2) All religions share a common moral code that reflects similar, if not identical, values for human behavior. For all practical purposes, the basic moral laws for how all members of any religion should behave in their respective communities are identical to the moral and ethical laws found in all other major religions and, for that matter, in any significant human social structure. It is a fundamental commonality that all religions prohibit the sins of murder, larceny, lying, brawling, and hatred, while encouraging the virtues of love, self-control, self-discipline, kindness, and helping the less fortunate.

    (3) All religions share a system of rituals designed to assist in educating the adherent in some fashion associated with the belief system.

    (4) All religions proclaim that the primary goal of the religion is for the salvation of the human soul, to obtain eternal fellowship (heaven) and not separation (hell) with God(s) or some other supreme sublime force in the afterlife.

Works vs. Grace

Since all religions share these commonalities, does that mean that "all roads lead to Rome?" What are the differences? The only issue that sharply and forever divides the seven major religions rests in the mechanics of how one achieves the goal of obtaining this eternal relationship with God under the fourth commonality listed above. In this regard, there are two, and only two, diametrically opposed answers to how this is achieved—Plan A or Plan B.

    Plan A is the most predominate religious view and asserts that salvation is worked for by a system of human merit. Plan B is the antithesis of Plan A and asserts that salvation is provided by God through a system of unmerited grace. Hence, the choice is either the grace-religion of Plan B or Plan A's works-religion.

    Those religions that teach that the mechanics by which man achieves eternal union with God via human merit, effort, or works (human morality coupled with the performance of various rituals) are properly classified as a works-religion, Plan A. All religions except Biblical Christianity fall into the camp of Plan A.[9]

Because it is a progressive belief system, works-religion provides no guarantee of acceptance or salvation while the adherent is living in his mortal body; there will be an evaluation process called a "judgment" where the good and bad deeds of the individual are weighed by God. If the supplicant is deemed worthy by his good works then admission to heaven is granted. If deemed not worthy, separation from God in hell.

In contrast, Biblical Christianity rejects the concept that man can ever achieve relationship with perfect God based on any system of morality, ritual, or any other system of human effort. Christian dogma states that relationship with God is automatically and irrevocably granted in one moment in time when the believer accepts the salvation work that the God/man, Jesus Christ, performed on the cross in AD 30. Christ took all humanity's sins into His own physical body—past, present, and future—and was judged by God the Father for them (1 *Peter* 2:24). Entrance into Plan B is by a simple, singular, act of non-meritorious faith alone in Christ alone (Acts 16:30). Non-progressive from top to bottom, God does all the work, man only accepts the results. Salvation is guaranteed at the moment of belief in Christ regardless of the past, present, or subsequent morality or immorality of the adherent.

Finally, "there is nothing new under the sun."[10] No human has ever had an original thought in terms of the basic underpinnings of life, nor will they. For instance, you tell me your thoughts, and I can point historically to where they have already been. While people can have mechanical thoughts that are novel, e.g., inventing a widget, or making a widget better, the philosophical and religious thoughts were here before we were born and will be here after we are dead. As demonstrated, in terms of religion there are only two basic options to consider. The issue is not that you will think a new thought in terms of religion, you won't. The only issue is what side

---

9. For a short comparison *see* Jeffrey F. Addicott, *The Misuse of Religion in the Global War on Terrorism*, 7 BARRY LAW REVIEW 109 (2006).
10. *Ecclesiastes* 1:4–11.

of the fence you will choose to line up on. Human volition is the key, it has been so since the beginning. This is the crux of freedom of religion. Christians celebrate it, Islamists hate it.

Chapter 6

Islam

"We must be aware that whenever Islam is transformed into an ideology, it becomes narrow and restricted, constrained by ideological limits and political reforms."[1]

—Ahmad Syafii Maarif

Islam is properly classified as a works-religion. It was not the first works-religion to appear in human history and it may or may not be the last. As with all works-religions, Islam demands progression and process with the adherent's life always subject to improvement, preparing for the final evaluation before God at the Judgment Seat of Allah.

Islam was introduced into the Middle East in the seventh century AD by an Arab named Abu al-Qasim Muhammad (570–632).[2] Muhammad was born into the Koreish tribe in Mecca, a prosperous city on the caravan route between the Mediterranean and the Indian Ocean in what is now Saudi Arabia. Although he was orphaned young and grew up poor and disadvantaged, Muhammad found work in the caravan business where he worked as a camel

---

1. THE ILLUSION OF AN ISLAMIC STATE 14 (H.E. Kyai Haji Abdurrahman, ed., 2011).
2. *See generally* Steven J. Rosen, INTRODUCTION TO THE WORLD'S MAJOR RELIGIONS (2006).

driver and then manager. In his profession he was exposed to many different people to include Jews, followers of Zoroastrianism, and Christians. At the age of 25 he married his first wife, a wealthy older Jewish widow named Khadija and entered a life of ease.

Freed from the need to work, Muhammad spent long hours in a mountain cave outside the city as was the practice of many other "holy" men in Mecca, a city known for its polytheism. In 610, Muhammad's spiritual expeditions climaxed with a vision in which Muhammad claimed that the angel Gabriel summoned him to be the last prophet to mankind, following Moses, Abraham, and Jesus (*see* Koran 96:1–5). Muhammad's wife, Khadija, convinced him that he was not possessed by a desert *jinn* (a malevolent supernatural creature). Muhammad proclaimed that Allah, one of the gods worshipped in Mecca, was the only god in existence and that all the other gods were false. An illiterate, Muhammad attracted a small band of followers who documented everything he said as the visions periodically continued.

At the age of forty Muhammad began to preach the religion of Islam in public, only to be greeted with skepticism and hostility by the ruling merchants of Mecca. Islam's monotheism deeply threatened the revenue stream that came to Mecca from the many pilgrimages to its 360 religious shrines.

After 12 years in Mecca, Muhammad was able to attract only about 100 followers. In 622, at the age of 52, he learned that he had gained some dedicated followers about 280 miles north in the rival caravan city of Yathrib, later named Medina. They needed a strong leader and were willing to accept Muhammad's Islam. The authorities in Mecca heard of Muhammad's plan to go to Yathrib and tried to prevent him from leaving the city, but were unsuccessful. Muhammad's transfer of venue in 622 is called the *hijira* (the flight) and marks the beginning of the Islamic calendar.

War soon followed between Muhammad's followers and Mecca. The first battle of significance took place in 624 and is known as the Battle of Badr. Muhammad's army, ill-trained and outnumbered, was nevertheless successful. Being victorious in this pitched battle provided inspiration throughout the entire war, and was also seen as an omen of Allah's support for their cause. After a series of violent and bloody fights between Muhammad and Mecca lasting several years, Muhammad took the city of Mecca by strong arm with a force of 10,000 and those who were not killed, converted to Islam. From Mecca, the new religion spread rapidly, primarily on the wings of military expansionism. During this military phase of Muhammad's life, the Muslims fought scores of bloody military battles that Muhammad either attended, fought in, or sent others to fight while he remained at Medina. Furthermore, Muhammad personally beheaded many hundreds of captives.[3] The battle cry heard on many a field of Muslim conquest was "*Allah-u-akbar*" which translated means "God is greater."[4]

When Muhammad died in 632, he left behind a battle-hardened army, ready to move into all parts of the known world. A disagreement about who should be the legitimate successor (a blood relative or not) led to a split in the religion, which exists today—Sunni and Shia. Today, over 80 percent of Muslims are Sunni. Muhammad's primary military chief, a father-in-law and longtime confidant, Abu Bakr (Abdullah ibn Abi Quhaafah), swiftly took control of the ever-expanding Islamic army and violently crushed all opposition to his claim as successor. Abu Bakr was the first Muslim *caliph* (supreme leader) and launched his Islamic forces across Arabia, winning battle after battle in the name of the new religion. Abu Bakr only lived two years after the death of Muhammad, but he set in motion a military tsunami that would not stop until the Muslim caliphate became one of the largest empires in history. Under Abu Bakr's short reign two goals were reached: (1) Islamic armies successfully conquered the entire Arabian Peninsula and converted the people to Islam, and (2) the first written version of the Koran was produced.

Under the second caliph, Umar ibn Al-Khattab (586–644), Muslim armies conquered Syria (AD 634), Iraq (636), Egypt (639), and Persia (642). In short order, Islam next grabbed Cyprus (647),

3. *See* Ibn Ishaq, THE LIFE OF MUHAMMAD (2002).
4. According to eyewitnesses at the scene of the *Charlie Hebdo* attack in Paris, the jihadists screamed that phrase repeatedly. *See* Dan Bilefsky and Maia De La Baume, *Terrorists Strike Charlie Hebdo Newspaper in Paris,* NEW YORK TIMES, January 17, 2015, at A1.

Tunisia and parts of Afghanistan (670), Rhodes (672), North Africa (700), lands adjacent to the western Chinese border (715), and Morocco (722).

By 710, the Arab Muslims had even entered Spain, only to be turned back from France by the Frankish ruler Charles Martel (688–741) and his Teutonic knights at the Battle of Tours in 732. Certainly, however, the Muslim caliphate was impressive at its peak, with many of the conquered people content to serve as second class citizens and pay the *jizya* (a special added tax for non-Muslims under Muslim control).[5] At its peak Islam encompassed all the Middle East, North Africa, southwest Asia, and parts of Europe.

In 1299 the Muslim, Ottoman Turks transformed the caliphate into the Ottoman Empire, but in 100 years the tide began to turn. In 1571 the Turks were defeated by the Italians and Austrians as the Muslim army and navy tried to cross the Mediterranean to attack southern Europe in the Battle of Lapanto. Then, in 1683 the Turkish forces were defeated at the Battle of Vienna by German and Polish forces. By the time the *sultan* of the Ottoman Empire sided with Germany in World War I, the caliphate was a mere shell of its former power. With the defeat of Germany, the Ottoman Empire was divided up with only what is modern day Turkey remaining.

Desiring to modernize his people, the new Turkish leader, Mustafa Ataturk, abolished the caliphate in 1922 and imposed secular law in Turkey in 1924. Ataturk's reforms enraged many strict constructionist Muslims and the movement to reestablish the Muslim caliphate and restore Sharia Law sprang up in 1928 with the formation of the Muslim Brotherhood under an Egyptian named Hassan al-Banna.

Islam's Requirements

The Koran,[6] along with the authentic prophetic narrations known as *hadith*, are the two most fundamental and important sources of guid-

---

5.   Mark S. Pfeiffer, TRUE JIHAD 23 (2013) (only Muslims could have authority over non-Muslims).
6.   All translations herein are from M.A.S. Abdel Haleem, THE QUR'AN (2004).

ance for Muslims. Both are central to the Islamic faith. The Koran contains all that Allah commands the follower to do and the hadith, also called the *sunnah* (path), concentrates on what Muhammad said and did during his life. Because many different people wrote down the words and actions of Muhammad during his life (sometimes from 3rd or 4th party sources), there are numerous hadiths and not all are given equal weight due to questions of authenticity. For certain, to be a labeled a genuine or authentic hadith it cannot contradict anything that is written in the Koran. Accordingly, Islamic schools of jurisprudence (*fiqh*) developed early on in order to provide official guidance on matters of interpretation and authenticity. These rulings quickly led to the formation of Sharia Law.

Koran comes from the word *al-qur'an*, meaning "recitation" in Arabic. The Koran is divided into 114 *suras*, or chapters. The chapters are not placed in a chronological order, but are categorized by specific topical themes such as "woman" or "repentance," etc. The chapters are further distinguished as being Meccan (the early part of Muhammad's revelations from the city of Mecca) or Medinan (the later part of Muhammad's revelations from the city of Median).

Muslims acknowledge that the Bible's Old and New Testaments are also divine, but believe that Christians and Jews altered the original text. (Considering that nine different men independently wrote the New Testament letters well within a fifty year span, this position is historically untenable). Jews and Christians are called People of the Book (the Bible) and all others of different religious beliefs are called idolaters.[7] All are infidels.

The follower of Islam is required to follow both the Koran and the sunnah. These are the gold standards for the followers of Islam.[8] The Koran 33:21 states that Muhammad was the perfect example of what a Muslim should be, and should be closely emulated.

---

7. *See generally* I.A. Ibrahim, A Brief Illustrated Guide to Understanding Islam 47–49 (1996).

8. *See* Mustafa Al-Sibai, *The Farewell Pilgrimage*, in The Biography of Allah's Prophet: Lessons And Examples 135-139 (Ghassan Abdel Fattah & Carlo Shariffa trans., 1993).

The religion has what are called the Five Pillars of Islam (as well as the Six Pillars of Faith). The pillars focus on various rituals and beliefs that every Muslim must accept and perform. In general terms, to be a Muslim requires the following:

(1) One must confess the core Islamic beliefs in the proper manner. The *shahada*, that Allah is god and that Muhammad the Prophet is his messenger: *"La ilaha illa Allah; Muhammad rasul Allah."* Although Islam recognizes that there have been other prophets before him, e.g., Moses and Jesus, Muhammad is the culmination and no legitimate prophet will ever succeed him. So, while Muslims reject the Jesus of the Bible as the promised Son of God and Messiah who died on the cross for sin and promises to return in the future to the world (Koran 5:73–75), some Muslim Sunnis do look for a special *Mahdi* to appear to usher in an apocalyptic end of the world and the final conquest for Allah. Some Shia have a similar concept of the end times and look for the return of a "missing" twelfth Imam to the earth (they are called Twelvers).

(2) One must pray in a particular manner that requires the faithful to prostrate himself in the direction of Mecca five times a day—*salat*. A caller delivers the call to prayer from a tall tower, a symbol to all that the nation is strictly tied to a communion with Allah and to a strict social brotherhood.

(3) Paying *zakat*. One must give money to the poor and to the religious organization in compliance with a set mathematical formula. The Koran is explicit on this matter; annually, two and one-half percent of the Muslim's property must be given to the poor.

(4) One must fast (*sawm; siyyam*) once each year, during the month of *Ramadan*. Ramadan is Islam's holy month. It is considered holy because it is the month Muhammad claimed to have had his first revelation, and the month Muhammad made his *hijra* (migration) from Mecca to Medina. From dawn until the sun sets, Muslims are not allowed to partake in food, drink, smoking, or sexual relations.

(5) One must go on a sacred pilgrimage; the greatest—required for all during their lifetime, if at all physically or financially possible—is the trip to Mecca. The annual pilgrimage to Mecca is called the *hajj*. The associated rituals include such things as: wearing the *ihram* (an unsewn cloth symbolizing the equality of all believers); circumambulation of the *ka'aba*; standing at the plain of *Arafat*; spending the night at *Muzdalifa*; throwing stones at three symbols of Satan; the sacrifice of an animal at *Mina*; drinking water from the well of *Zamzam*; and the performance of two cycles of prayer at the Station of Abraham.[9]

Sharia Law

Then there is Sharia Law, a principal legal foundation in most Muslim-majority countries that was formulated early on by recognized Islamic scholars.[10] As a works-religion, the Koran and sunnah set out the mandates for Muslims to perform, such as obeying certain morality codes, praying, fasting, paying zakat, making the hajj, etc. But Sharia alone instructs the Muslim in *how* to accomplish these activities. Sharia Law details how an adherent correctly practices Islam. Obeying Sharia Law pleases Allah and more importantly it provides a standard for evaluation at Allah's Judgment Seat as to whether the individual Muslim will go to heaven or be cast into hell.

---

9.   Every Muslim who is physically and economically capable is required to make a pilgrimage to Mecca. When Muslims reach Mecca they are expected to dress in simple white robes to symbolize unity. This is known as the cleansing period or *ihram*. The great pilgrimage is not just a journey, but a very specific ritual that must take place. Muslims circle the Ka'aba (the sacred meteoric stone of the Islamic faith) seven times, run seven times between the hills of Safa and Marwa, travel thirteen miles to the plains of Arafat, and then go to Mina to cast stones in an act symbolizing the rejection of evil by Abraham. Pilgrims then make an animal sacrifice and return to circle the Ka'aba once more, completing the *hajj*.

10. See *Sharia in American Courts: The Expanding Incursion of Islamic Law in the U.S. Legal System*, CENTER FOR SECURITY POLICY, January 5, 2015.

Sharia directly and deeply applies to all aspects of life with moral and legal codes and taboos to instruct on personal affairs, social affairs, and political affairs. In Muslim countries such as Saudi Arabia, Kuwait, Bahrain, Yemen, and the United Arab Emirates, Sharia is officially declared to be the source, or a source of the country's law. In other Muslim nations such as Pakistan, Iran, and Iraq it is also forbidden to enact any legislation that is in opposition to Islam.[11]

The oil-rich nation of Saudi Arabia employs one of the strictest interpretations of Sharia Law. Women are under the guardianship of male relatives at all times, cannot drive vehicles, and must be completely covered in public. Drinking intoxicants, gambling, eating pork, and unlawful sexual relations (a man can be married to several wives), are just a few of the prohibitions of Sharia, which bear most heavily on the conduct of women. According to a 2013 Pew Survey, "74 percent of Muslims in Egypt feel that Sharia should be the 'country's official legal code,' and an equal majority say it should apply to non-Muslims as well as Muslims."[12]

As a law professor, I am often asked about Sharia Law and whether it is compatible with Western values and our Anglo-Saxon legal traditions. My answer is always to first point to the pronouncement of the leading international court in the world, the European Court of Human Rights (*Cour Europeenne des droits de l'homme*); not a right leaning court by any stretch of the imagination. In a landmark case issued from Strasbourg in 2003, *Refah Partisi and Others v. Turkey*,[13] the Court unequivocally ruled that Sharia Law is absolutely incompatible with the fundamental principles of freedom and democracy:

---

11. *See* Tony Johnson, *Islam: Governing Under Sharia*, COUNCIL ON FOREIGN RELATIONS, July 25, 2014.

12. Loren Thompson, *Five Reasons the ISIS Fight Isn't About Islam*, FORBES, February 26, 2015, *available at* http://www.forbes.com/sites/lorenthompson/2015/02/26/five-reasons-the-isis-fight-isnt-about-islam/2/.

13. *Refah Partisi v. Turkey* [GC], no. 41340/98, 41342/98, 41343/98 and 41344/98, February 13, 2003.

(b) Sharia …

The Court concurs in the Chamber's view that sharia is incompatible with the fundamental principles of democracy, as set forth in the Convention [Convention for Human Rights and Fundamental Freedoms]: Like the Constitutional Court, the Court considers sharia, with faithfully reflects the dogma and divine rules laid down by religion … the introduction of Sharia, are difficult to reconcile with the fundamental principles of democracy … It is difficult to declare one's respect for democracy and human rights while at the same time supporting a regime based on sharia, which clearly diverges from Convention [on Human Rights] values, particularly with regard to its criminal law and criminal procedure, its rules on the legal status of women and the way it intervenes in all spheres of private and public life in accordance with religious precepts.

Of course, pointing out that Sharia is a horrendous construct that is incompatible with all concepts of democracy and freedom is rarely voiced in America. In fact, most Americans are totally ignorant of the content of Sharia Law and view it as a benign lifestyle code that Muslims should be encouraged to practice here in the United States. Nothing could be more false or ludicrous, particularly to those Americans that cherish the fundamental pillars of freedom and equality before the law upon which our nation was founded. To those who truly love freedom, denigrating the concept of Sharia law openly and often is not ethnocentric. As Edmund Burke put it, "all that is necessary for evil to triumph is for good men to do nothing." Indeed, even if the multiculturalism crowd in American doesn't get it, at least the Sultan of Brunei and his royal family know the heavy burden Sharia imposes on human freedom. In Brunei, Sharia Law is imposed on every human being living in the country except, of course, the Sultan and his royal family.[14]

---

14. See Emily Moulton, *Sex, Lies and Sharia Law: The Secret Life of the Sultan of Brunei*, HERALD SUN, April 27, 2015, at A4.

Jihad

Finally, there is the concept of *jihad* as a major component of Islam. Without question, in the discussion of terrorism, jihad is the most controversial aspect of Islam. Regardless of what individuals may want the word to mean—the literal translation is "striving to achieve a goal" or "struggle"[15]—a review of the authoritative Islamic sources clearly indicates that the primary meaning of jihad is "holy war," the requirement for the Muslim to take up arms and to do violence to others in order to defend or to spread the religion of Islam.

> The main motif of *jihad* in the *Hadith* is death on the battleground in the way of *Allah*, which leads, through an immediate passage, to paradise, and intends to cause a sacred wedding to the black-eyed virgins (*huris al-ayn*) as heavenly reward for the believer upon his heroic death.[16]

According to a detailed white paper prepared at the direction of the then Democratic majority U.S. Congress in 2010, the term jihadist (taken from the word jihad) describes an individual who employs the religion of Islam to justify the desire to establish a world which is governed by a Muslim civil and religious system known as a caliphate.[17] Someone engaged in jihad is called a *mujhad*, the plural of which is *mujahideen*. As will be explored at chapter 7 on radical Islam, this is a central doctrine for the radical Islamist and provides an alternative way to reach paradise if they should die in jihad.

It is incontrovertible that aggressive war in Islamic classic history is a fact and jihad served from the start as a powerful motivational tool for mobilizing the faithful to fight the infidels and expand the religion. Thus, of all the duties of the Muslim, jihad is considered the most noble.

---

15. For an excellent discussion on jihad and its origin in Islamic law *see* David Bukay, FROM MUHAMMAD TO BIN LADEN 45–75 (2008).

16. *Id.* at 61.

17. See Jerome P. Bjelopera, CONGRESSIONAL RESEARCH SERVICE, RL41416, AMERICAN JIHADIST TERRORISM: COMBATING A COMPLEX THREAT 1 (2010).

Illustrations of Islamists using the term jihad to unequivocally mean violence and killing for a holy mission are legion. In the words of one of the most recognized Arab leaders of the last 50 years,[18] the former President of the Palestinian Liberation Organization and of the Palestinian people, Yasser Arafat, jihad was for the killing of Jews.[19]

> We know only one word: *jihad, jihad, jihad*. When we stopped the intifada [the Palestinian leadership launched two major uprisings that murdered hundreds of Jews in Israel by terror suicide attacks], we did not stop the *jihad* for the establishment of a Palestinian State whose capital is Jerusalem. And we are now entering the phase of the great *jihad* prior to the establishment of an independent Palestinian State whose capital is Jerusalem.[20]

> "Struggle struggle, struggle, struggle. Combat, combat, combat, combat. *Jihad, jihad, jihad, jihad*."[21]

Then there is Osama bin Laden's view of jihad. In an audio message released several years after 9/11, bin Laden declared that all Muslims were required to wage jihad:

> It is the duty for the *Umma* [nation] with all its categories of men, women and youths, to give away themselves, their money, experiences and all types of material support... *jihad* today is an imperative for every Muslim. The Umma

---

18. *See* Jeffrey F. Addicott, *Using a Civil Suit to Punish/Deter Sponsors of Terrorism: Connecting Arafat and the PLO to the Terror Attacks of the Second Intifada*, 4 ST. JOHN'S JOURNAL OF INTERNATIONAL AND COMPARATIVE LAW (2014).
19. *See* Thomas X. Hammes, THE SLING AND THE STONE 111–129 (2004).
20. *In the Words of Arafat*, NEW YORK TIMES, August 4, 1997, at A1.
21. *Yasser Arafat Calls for Jihad, Struggle, and Combat*, PALESTINIAN MEDIA WATCH (Oct. 21, 1996), palwatch.org/main.aspx?fi=711&fld_id=5253 (providing a media clip from official Palestinian TV).

will commit sin if it did not provide adequate material support for *jihad*.[22]

The new leader of al-Qa'eda, Ayman al-Zawahiri, also interprets jihad to mean killing and aspiring to Allah's paradise:

> [America] reinforce your security measures. The Islamic nation which sent you the New York and Washington brigades [9/11 attacks] has taken the firm decision to send you successive brigades to sow death and aspire to paradise [by dying in jihad].[23]

To the Islamist, jihad is not murder at all, it is justified homicide which is commanded and condoned by Islam. In this light, many jihadists on trial for murder will assert that they are not guilty of murder as the killings were justified. The ten Muslim defendants convicted of attacking the Twin Towers in New York City in 1993 requested the federal trial court to consider their religious views as a defense to the terror attack. Their spiritual leader, Omar Abdel Rahman (the blind Sheikh) submitted lengthy offers of proof suggesting that their actions were justified and governed by Islamic law. These included:

> The five pillars or basic precepts of Islam [are] Faith, Prayer, Alms, Pilgrimage, and Fasting. Muslim clerics and scholars have preached about ... a Muslim's necessity to engage in jihad ... Jihad [had its] origins in Islam after Prophet Mohammed began preaching in the 7th Century ... Jihad is cast in the mold of a legal doctrine ... Jihad has come to mean ... the combating of oppression ... The Muslim community as a whole has a collective duty or obligation to engage in armed struggle in the path of God [which] must be organized and announced by a Caliph or Sultan. It is only when the enemy attacks Muslim territory that jihad becomes an

---

22. Peter L. Bergen, THE OSAMA BIN LADEN I KNOW (2006).
23. Ayman al-Zawahiri, *quoted in In Their Own Words*, CI Centre's Counterterrorism Studies, http://ctstudies.com/In_Their_Own_Words_1.html.

individual duty ... It is an individual obligation for able-bodied Muslims from all over to come to the aid of their brethren, [and] jihad is governed by a very clear set of rules such as an invitation to embrace Islam, treatment of prisoners, and division of spoils.[24]

The totalitarian regime of Iran regularly uses jihad coterminous with calls to kill Jews and Americans. At the annual Quds (Jerusalem) Day "Festival" in Iran, hundreds of thousands of Iranians parade in the streets of their capital Tehran each year carrying banners proclaiming "Death to Israel!" and "Death to America!" as they listen motivational to speeches by the mullahs and other leaders of the country. At the July 2015 event held just before Obama concluded a nuclear treaty that paved the way for Iran to get nuclear weapons, the President of Iran, Hassan Rouhani, wrote on his website: "With unity, resistance, *jihad*, and sacrifice, the Muslims, including the Palestinian people, will reach their goals [destroying Israel and taking Jerusalem]."[25] The top military aide to Supreme Leader Ayatollah Ali Kamenei echoed Rouhani by saying: "Muslim unity and continuation of armed jihad and the Islamic resistance of the Palestinian nation constitute the only strategy for saving and liberating the Holy Quds [Jerusalem]."[26] They mean jihad to mean aggressive violence!

Still, most Muslims today will assert that in the modern era jihad only speaks of an inner spiritual cleansing of wicked thoughts and deeds to improve one's life in preparation for the Judgment Seat of Allah. They call this *al-jihad al-akbar* (greater jihad) with warfare being *al-jihad al-asghar* (lesser jihad).

In addition, it is often noted that those Muslims who kill themselves in suicide attacks are destined to hell, as suicide is a grievous sin in Islamic theology.[27] The jihadist counters this contention by

---

24. *United States v. Rahman*, 189 F.3d 88 (2d Cir. 1999). Letter from Abdeen Jabara, counsel for Rahman, to Andrew C. McCarthy, Asst. U.S. Atty. (July 7, 1995).

25. Sohrab Ahmari, *Our Death-to-America Nuclear Negotiating Partners*, WALL STREET JOURNAL, July 11-12, 2015, at A9.

26. *Id.*

27. Shaul Shay, THE SHAHIDS 9-10 (2004).

pointing out that while suicide for personal reasons is a sin, self-sacrifice for the cause of Allah is a virtue commanded in the Koran. Those who die by killing themselves in jihad win the title of *shahid*, along with all the benefits in the afterlife. Those who die by killing themselves for personal reasons go to hell.

Just as personal suicide, a sin, is not the same as self-sacrifice for Allah in jihad, the idea of a greater jihad and lesser jihad is not a distinction that is widely recognized. The greater jihad idea originates from only a single late source (the eleventh century) by a single Islamic scholar named al-Khatib al-Baghdadiis, in his book *History of Baghdad*. This particular hadith was passed down through four people, the last being Layth. It says that when Muhammad returned from one of his many battles, he said: "You have arrived with an excellent arrival, you have come from the lesser jihad [the battle against non-Muslims] to the greater jihad—the striving of a servant [of Allah] against his desires."[28]

Not only does this hadith contradict the Koran, which disqualifies it immediately as genuine, it also stands in opposition to all Islamic schools of thought which predate it. Again, its power rests solely in the fact that it tells the uninformed what they want to hear, not what classic Islam really says.

Many non-Muslims like President Obama's senior counter-terrorism advisor, John Brennan, are eager to pick up on this greater jihad concept because it dovetails quite nicely with their desire to believe that no part of Islam can possibly command killing non-Muslims or apostates. For example, in a recent report issued by the International Centre for the Study of Radicalism and Political Violence (ICSR), jihad is self-defined by the authors as "an Islamic concept which means 'struggle' and can refer to all kinds of religiously inspired effort—be they spiritual, personal, political, or military."[29] Nevertheless, the report goes on to contradict itself about jihad. It labels Muslims that use violence in terror as "jihadists" practicing "jihadism," which obviously seems to be the primary connotation

---

28. *See* Imam al-Suyuti, 4 Fayd al-Qadir Sharh al-Jami al Saghir (Ed. Beirut: Dar al-Ma'rifah) 511.

29. Peter R. Neumann, *The New Jihadism: A Global Snapshot*, International Centre for the Study of Radicalism and Political Violence (2015).

of jihad. The report agrees that these "jihadists" interpret jihad to mean "fighting," and that "every able-bodied Muslim has an obligation to fulfill this duty" of killing the infidels and apostates.

Clearly, in order to find the original meaning of jihad it is necessary to go to the most authoritative sources of Islamic interpretation. In contrast to the popular non-violent view of jihad, the corpus of Islamic jurisprudence, which continues into the modern era, says otherwise. The standard majority definition of jihad is a call to violent behavior in spreading or protecting Islam and is found in all four major Sunni schools of Islamic jurisprudence—*Hanafi*, *Maliki, Shafi'i*, and *Hanbali*. In turn, the Shia school of *Shi'a Jafari* holds that jihad means using violence to fight and die for the cause of Islam.[30] Absolutely none of these schools make any reference whatsoever to the idea of a "greater jihad." All hold that jihad means violence by military conquest in Allah's name.

For instance, in the *Umdat al-Salik* (Reliance of the Traveler) from the Shafi'i school of Islam:

> Jihad means to war against non-Muslims, and is etymologically derived from the word *mujahada*, signifying warfare to establish religion ... Details concerning jihad are found in the accounts of the military expeditions of the Prophet [Muhammad].[31]

The Koran itself is replete with verses commanding violent jihad. Koran [Medinan] 8:39 unequivocally commands jihad as a permanent and overriding command for the Muslim to "fight them [non-Muslims] until there is no more persecution, and [your] worship is devoted to Allah alone."

> Prophet [Muhammad], work hard [jihad] against the unbelievers and the hypocrites, and be tough with them. Hell is their final home – an evil destination. Koran [Medinan] 9:73

30. For an excellent discussion *see* Daniel Akbari & Paul Tetreault, HONOR KILLING 35-36 (2014).
31. *Id.* at 9.

Jihad means literal physical violence and this is the duty of all Muslims. But Jihad can also be waged by providing material support. The Koran [Medinan] at 9:20 and 9:41 does promise Muslims that they will do well if they support jihad with their property.

As one would expect, the Koran also says that those Muslims that do not engage in jihad by fighting or providing material support (to include immigrating to non-Muslim lands in order to spread Islam) are inferior to Muslims that do.

> Those believers who stay at home, apart from those with an incapacity, are not equal to those who commit themselves and their possessions to striving [jihad] in God's way. God has raised such people to a rank above those who stay at home – although He has promised all believers a good reward, those who strive are favored with a tremendous reward above those who stay at home ... Koran [Medinan] 4:95

As popular as the vanilla wafer, greater jihad may seem to many as the preferable interpretation, the reality is that labeling the primary meaning of jihad as a self-improvement regime is untenable if you are a strict constructionist of Islamic teachings. Supported by only a single source arriving much later in chronology, the strict constructionist of Islam has no choice but to reject the idea of the so-called greater jihad. One can certainly argue that violent jihad is no longer relevant in this modern era and has fallen into abeyance, but the argument is hardly based on religious authoritative text or traditions.

Then there is the concept of offensive and defensive jihad. In normative Islamic tradition there is a distinction made between offensive and defensive jihad. Offensive jihad is a community obligation to be waged against the infidel by means of violence in order to expand Islam. Since from the beginning the goal of Islam was to spread across the world, this was the primary usage of jihad. Defensive jihad emerged as an individual obligation to fight along with the entire Muslim community when the infidel attacks the *dar al-Islam* (areas under Muslim control).[32] Naturally, this distinction quickly blurs as Islamists all claim that they are merely defending themselves and Islam when they kill.

Finally, there is an added difficulty in making assessments about the correct meaning of jihadi due to the Muslim doctrine of *taqiyya*, which allows Muslims to act or speak in a deceptive manner as long as they remain true to core Islamic principles in their mind. In some instances of discussion there is no way to know if taqiyya is being employed, in others it is very clear, e.g., the Iranians will never keep their promises under any nuclear deal with the United States.[33]

> The believers [Muslims] should not make the disbelievers [non-Muslims] their allies rather than other believers—anyone who does such a thing will isolate himself completely from Allah—except when you need to protect yourselves from them [you can then practice deception]. Koran [Medinan] 3:28-29

> Allah and His messenger are released from [treaty] obligations to the polytheists. Koran [Medinan] 9:3

> With the exception of those who are forced to say they do not believe, although their hearts remain firm in faith, those who reject Allah after believing in Him and open their hearts to disbelief will have the wrath of God upon them and a grievous punishment awaiting them. Koran 16:106

> He [Allah] has ordained a way for you [believers] to release you from [your] oaths. Koran [Medinan] 66:2

---

32. David Bukay, FROM MUHAMMAD TO BIN LADEN 78–79 (2008).
33. *See* Dore Gold, THE RISE OF NUCLEAR IRAN (2009).

So, when certain Muslim apologists vehemently declare that jihad has nothing to do with "holy war" and violence the knowledge-
able observer is left scratching his head. Based on the documentary
and historical evidence at hand, it is clear that they are lying under
taqiyya to advance the spread of Islam.

Almost the Bottom Line on Islam

In conclusion, Muhammad founded a works-religion that prescribes
for the adherent an extremely strict moral, social, political, and legal code, coupled with a series of demanding rituals. In contrast to
Jesus of Nazareth, Muhammad stressed that he was not divine; he
was only a flawed human whom God had chosen to be the messenger of divine revelations. His message was that the adherent must
precisely follow all of the Islamic moral laws and codes of behavior
to include jihad and then stand at a final judgment tribunal conducted by Allah where the follower will be evaluated as to whether
he is deemed worthy enough to enter heaven. The alternative is to
spend eternity in the fires of hell with all infidels.

> On that Day, the weighing of deeds will be true and just:
> those who's good deeds are heavy on the scales will be the
> ones to prosper, and those whose good deeds are light will
> be the ones who have lost their souls through their wrongful
> rejection of Our messages. Koran [Meccan] 7:8-9

> [T]he one whose good deeds are heavy on the scales will
> have a pleasant life [in paradise], but the one whose good
> deeds are light will have the Bottomless Pit for his home
> – what will explain to you what that is? – A blazing fire.
> Koran [Meccan] 101:6-11

> We will set up scales of justice for the Day of Resurrection
> [the soul is in a resurrection body] so that no one can be
> wronged in the least, and if there should be even the weight

of a mustard seed, We shall bring it out – We take excellent
account. Koran [Meccan] 21:47

Interestingly, even the founder of the religion, Muhammad, did
not know if he was going to go to heaven when he died. Speaking about that time when he would stand before Allah's judgment
scales, Muhammad remarked in a hadith: "By Allah, though I am
the Apostle of Allah, yet do I not know what Allah will do to me."[34]
In the Koran, Muhammad warned:

I am not an innovation among the Messengers, and I know
not what shall be done with me or with you, I only follow
what is revealed to me; I am only a clear warner. Koran
[Meccan] 46:9

34. SAHIH AL-BUKHARI, Volume 5, Book 58, MERITS OF THE HELPERS IN MADINAH,
Number 266.

Chapter 7

Radical Islam

*"The attacks made people think about ... **true Islam**, which benefited them greatly."*[1]

—Osama bin Laden

We have already seen that President Obama consistently refused to use the term radical Islam to describe those who murder and commit atrocities in the name of Allah. We have also noted that those who fall into the category of radical Islam take a strict constructionist view of the Koran with particular devotion to the mandate of jihad and a zeal to follow the example set by Muhammad in punctilious detail. To be sure, even if one were to discount all that is written in the Koran, sunnah, or Sharia, actions speak louder than words and the actions of Muhammad make it abundantly certain that brutal aggressive violence to include murder was a key component in how Islam was disseminated. In fact, as a military commander, Muhammad excelled.

The goal of radical Islam is nothing less than world domination where the supremacy of Islam is implemented across the world.

---

1. The Global War on Terrorism: The First 100 Days, U.S. Department of State, http://2001-2009.state.gov/s/ct/rls/wh/6947.htm. *See also* Peter L. Bergen, THE OSAMA BIN LADEN I KNOW (2006).

These radical Islamic groups divide the world into two camps according to the dictates of Islam—*dar-al-Islam* (house of Islam), where peace reigns under true Islamic rule, and the *dar-al-Harb* (house of War), all the rest. According to the Koran, the primary means to achieve the goal of conquest for Allah is not by peaceful persuasion of the efficacy of Islamic theology but by violence and terror firmly rooted to specific traditions and texts of Islam. The script on the black flag of ISIS is the Muslim shahada: *La ilaha illa Allah; Muhammad rasul Allah* (Allah is god and Muhammad the Prophet is his messenger), leaving no doubt that they are rooted in Islam. We call them *radical* Islam, they call themselves the *true* Islam. In the book, *Islam and Terrorism*, the author understands that the strict constructionist text matters:

> In Islamic Law there are only two types of nations – a nation that is of the house of Islam or a nation that is of the house of war. We all know that America and most of the European countries are not 'the house of Islam,' meaning they do not live by the Islamic law; therefore, they are the 'house of war;' Muslims who have any sense of loyalty to Islam will have a hard time justifying loyalty to their country if that country is not Islamic. The true Muslim believes the whole world is his home and that he is commanded to submit the world to the authority of Islam. A sincere believer of Islam will not die for a patch of dirt called the homeland, but he is willing to die for Islam and Islamic holy practices."[2]

The prime weapon of choice to attack their enemies is by the so-called "suicide" terror attack. In most instances, the *mujhad* (martyr) self-detonates some sort of an explosive device striking death and fear in the heart of the enemies of Allah, as he bravely lays down his life. As previously discussed, self-sacrifice for jihad is permissible and even preferred according to Islam, while suicide, out of selfish considerations, is a grievous sin which brings the punishment of hell fire at Allah's Judgement Seat. Dying in the cause of Allah is never suicide, it is mujhad.

2.   Mark A. Gabriel, Islam and Terrorism 47 (2002).

From a military perspective martyrdom attacks have many advantages to include the following:

1. The terror attack is inexpensive and simple to do.
2. The jihadist can choose the when and where of the terror attack to ensure maximum effect.
3. Because there is no exit strategy, the jihadist cannot be interrogated for intelligence about the organization.
4. Terror attacks by means of self-sacrifice cause greater levels of fear in the target population.

In terms of authorizing martyrdom attacks, both Shia and Sunni brands of radical Islam are complicit. Imam Khomeini and other Shia clerics issued numerous formal religious rulings during the 1980–1988 war with Iraq for their people to sacrifice themselves and earn the title of *shahid* (another Islamic term for martyr with emphasis on being a witness to the faith). Thousands heeded the call, including their own children sent to detonate the Iraqi land mines on the front lines of battle.

Numerous Sunni clerics have also issued religious decrees authorizing martyrdom. One of the earlier decrees was issued on Qatar television in 1996, by Sheikh al-Kardawi, a leading cleric in the Muslim world. Kardawi affirmed that suicide terror attacks on Jewish civilians in that year where not suicide but "Jihad for Allah."[3] Kardawi condemned all Muslim clerics that rejected martyrdom as agents of secular regimes and "not binding religious authority."

The rise of radical Islam in the modern era is traced back almost 100 years ago to the collapse of the last caliphate under the Ottoman Turks in 1922. Following World War I, most of the Middle East fell under the rule of autocrats and dictators of one sort or the other. Radical Islamists like the Muslim Brotherhood[4] longed for a return to power under the strict precepts of Islam and fomented unrest wherever and whenever they could, using attacks on Western interests and Israel as a rallying cry for all Muslims to perform jihad.

3. Shaul Shay, THE SHAHIDS 9–10 (2004).
4. *See* Lawrence Wright, THE LOOMING TOWER (2006) (following the impact of the group in radical Islam).

The first major victory for radical Islam in the modern era came not with the Sunni based version but with the Shia radicals in Iran. In a pattern that would repeat itself in the "Arab Spring" demonstrations of 2009–2014, the people's uprising against the U.S. friendly Shah of Iran was quickly co-opted by the radical Islamists under the vicious Ayatollah Ruhollah Khomeini who had been exiled in France. Khomeini and his Muslim radicals took control of the military and government and set up a system of Sharia Law where the nation was ruled by the religious mullahs and ayatollahs under the façade of a "parliamentary system." In quick step, Iran openly exported its influence by means of terror to many parts of the Middle East with its tentacles reaching to Lebanon and the creation of the terrorist group Hezbollah. Iran's ultimate prize, of course, is the acquisition of nuclear weapons.

Sunni radical Islam found its first real success in fighting the Soviets in Afghanistan from 1979–1992 which gave rise to al-Qa'eda. While they failed to win power in Algeria in the 1992–2004 conflict, they would find an opportunity in Iraq in the aftermath of the 2003 American defeat of Saddam Hussein. Chapters 9 and 10 discuss the post-2003 era of Sunni radical Islam under al-Qa'eda and ISIS.

The predominantly young Muslim males are the main foot soldiers of radical Islam. They are lured into death (euphemistically called martyrdom) by the religious promise of automatically securing a place in *jannah* (paradise) for themselves where they will receive 72 *houris* (gazelle-eyed virgin companions) and the expectation that they will be allowed to choose friends and family members to join them in heaven.[5] The Muslim clerics extrapolate this belief from Islamic hadiths. In fact, the Koran, which does promise paradise to those who "slay and are slain" for Allah (Koran 9:111), also promises one or more houris for all who go to paradise (by means of the Judgment Seat of Allah). These *haura* are described throughout

---

5. *See* Garret Machine, *Hunting Suicide Bombers,* THE COUNTERTERRORIST, April/May 2015, at 8 (describing how Hamas would recruit young males and "introduce them to the ways of the jihad… and of course the most ridiculous part: the 72 virgins.")

the Koran as supernaturally created companions that are "chaste" (Koran 37:48; 55:56), "eyes like pearls" (Koran 56:22-23), "full-breasted" (Koran 78:33), etc.

Perhaps one of the most chilling revelations of the vicious mindset of radical Islam is found in an Osama bin Laden videotape, released to the public on December 13, 2001. The tape clearly illustrates the mindset of radical Islam. In the conversation between bin Laden and Sheikh Khaled al-Harbi (who surrendered to Saudi officials in 2004) regarding the attacks of September 11, 2001, numerous references are made to "Allah," "Muhammad," the *"fiqh* [holy war] of Muhammad," and so on. At one point, bin Laden boasts that the attacks were beneficial to a true understanding of Islam. "The attacks made people think about ... *true* Islam, which benefited them greatly." The video closes with the guest praising bin Laden in the name of Allah, "By Allah my Shaykh [bin Laden]. We congratulate you for the great work. Thank Allah."[6]

Their true Islam seeks to kill the *kafir*, or unbeliever. After all, since the kafir will burn in the fires of hell in the hereafter, he deserves death in this present life.

The disbelievers – those of the People of the Book [Jews and Christians] who disbelieve and the idolaters [all poly-theists] – will have the Fire of Hell, there to remain forever. They are the worst of creation. Koran [Medinan] 98:6

In tandem with the kafir, radical Islam also targets for death the *murtad* (apostate) which is a Muslim that makes a conscious decision to abandon Islam in word or deed. Along with radical Islamists, many non-radicalized Muslims agree with the general consensus set throughout Islamic history that actual apostasy is a crime punishable by death under Sharia Law.[7]

---

6. The Global War on Terrorism: The First 100 Days, U.S. Department of State, http://2001-2009.state.gov/s/ct/rls/wh/6947.htm. *See also* Peter L. Bergen, THE OSAMA BIN LADEN I KNOW (2006).

7. *See generally* S.A. Rahman, *Punishment of Apostasy in Islam*, INSTITUTE OF ISLAMIC CULTURE (2006).

[T]he repentance of those who, having believed, then increase in their disbelief, will not be accepted. They are the
ones who have gone astray: Those who disbelieve and die
disbelievers will not be saved even if they offer enough
gold to fill the entire earth. Agonizing torment is in store for
them, and there will be no one to help them. Koran [Medi-
nan] 3:90–91

In July 2015, ISIS released a video showing a man accused of *ridda*
(defection from Islam) having his head cut off and his body crucified on a Syrian city wall.

There are numerous terrorist organizations that fit the mold of
radical Islam. The State Department's 2014 list of foreign terrorist
organizations (FTO) are foreign terror groups that are designated
by the Secretary of State in accordance with Section 219 of the
Immigration and Nationality Act, as amended.[8] These FTO designations contain 59 groups from around the world. The vast majority, at least 45, of these FTOs are considered radical Islam. The
list includes: Abu Nidal Organization, Abu Sayyaf Group, Abdallah Azzam Brigades, Al-Shabaab, Al-Aqsa Martyrs Brigade, Army
of Islam, Ansar al-Islam, Ansar al-Dine, Ansaru, Al-Mulathamun
Battalion, Ansar al-Sharia in Benghazi, Ansar al-Sharia in Tunisia,
Ansar Bayt al-Maqdis, Al-Nusra Front, Asbat al-Ansar, Al-Qa'ida,
Al-Qa'ida in the Lands of the Islamic Maghreb, Al-Qa'ida in the
Arabian Peninsula, Ansar al-Islam, Armed Islamic Group, Boko
Haram, Gama'a al-Islamiyya, Hamas,[9] Harakat ul-Jihad-i-Islami,
Haqqani Network, Hezbollah, Islamic State of Iraq and the Levant,

---

8. Foreign Terrorist Organizations (FTOs) are designated by the Secretary
of State in accordance with section 219 of the Immigration and Nationality
Act (INA). The organization must engage in terrorist activity, as defined in
section 212 (a)(3)(B) of the INA (8 U.S.C. § 1182(a)(3)(B)), or terrorism, as
defined in section 140(d)(2) of the Foreign Relations Authorization Act, Fiscal Years 1988 and 1989 (22 U.S.C. § 2656f(d)(2)), or retain the capability
and intent to engage in terrorist activity or terrorism.
9. *See* Matthew Levitt, Hamas: Politics, Charity, and Terrorism in the Service
of Jihad (2006) (describing the origin and purpose of the terrorist organization).

Islamic Jihad Union, Jemahh Anshorut Tauhid, Jaish-e-Mohammed, Jundallah, Jemaah Islamiya, Kata'ib Hizballah, Islamic Movement of Uzbekistan, Indian Mujahidin, Lashkar-e-Tayyiba, Libyan Islamic Fighting Group, Lashkar-e-Jhangvi, Mujahedin Shura Council in the Environs of Jerusalem, Palestinian Islamic Jihad, Palestinian Liberation Front, PFLP-General Command, Popular Front for the Liberation of Palestine, and Tehrik-e Taliban Pakistan.

Many of these radical Islamic groups are indoctrinated with extreme Islamic fundamentalism spewed from radicalized *madrasas* (religious schools) which operate with impunity in such countries as Saudi Arabia, Pakistan, and Iran. In the case of many militant Islamic terrorist organizations, direct links have been established to various *Deobandi* religious schools, which are known for openly advocating the most violent forms of terrorism against Western interests.

It is not uncommon to see religious sermons on promoting the virtues of jihad in many parts of the Middle East, particularly during periods of open conflict with Israel. A sampling of some religious pronouncements from the ongoing call for the destruction of the Jews in Israel shows that in their minds and hearts they are rooted in Islam.

In 2001, Sheikh Ikrima Sabri, the Mufti of Jerusalem who was on the Palestinian Authority (PA) payroll, verbally praised the use of suicide attacks against civilians, promoting "jihad and martyrdom."[10] In June 2001, one sermon broadcast by the PA station stated:

> Blessings to whoever waged *jihad* for the sake of Allah; blessings to whoever raided for the sake of Allah; blessings to whoever put a belt of explosives on his body or on his sons' and plunged into the midst of the Jews.[11]

---

10. *The Highest Ranking Palestinian Authority Cleric; In Praise of Martyrdom Operations*, MEMRI (June 11, 2001), http://www.memri.org/report/en/0/0/0/0/0/0/466.htm.
11. *Friday Sermon on PA TV: Calling for Suicide Bombings*, MEMRI (June 13, 2001), http://www.memri.org/report/en/0/0/0/0/0/0/467.htm.

Another sermon on the official PA station asserted, "We must educate our children on the love of jihad for the sake of Allah and the love of fighting for the sake of Allah."[12] Yet another sermon broadcast by PA TV said there would be "blessings for whoever has saved a bullet in order to stick it in a Jew's head..."[13]

In addition, radical clerics in Western nations also preach this brand of hate to their followers. For instance, many of the Muslim terrorists associated with the July 7 and 21, 2005, bombings in London had direct links to the infamous Findsbury Park Mosque in London that preached jihad. The Muslim cleric Abuy Hamza al-Masri was subsequently arrested on suspicion of terrorism links.

With the meteoric rise of ISIS, the number of adherents of radical Islam is large and growing, easily reaching into the millions if one counts the messianic strain of Twelver Shiism in Iran (belief that the twelfth legitimate successor of the prophet Muhammad who is said to have disappeared in the tenth century will return to reign over a world where Islam is universal). Syria, Iraq, Yemen, Libya, Sudan, Nigeria, Tunisia, Somalia, Sudan, Pakistan, Algeria, Egypt, Jordan, Saudi Arabia, and other Middle Eastern nations teem with adherents and sympathizers of radical Islam.

The most repulsive hallmark associated with the spread of radical Islam is not the operation of religious terror schools for the adult jihadists, but rather the established methodology of inculcating an ideology of religious hatred into the minds of innocent children from the moment of birth. In the homes, communities, and the madrasas, countless numbers of innocent children are brainwashed each and every day of their lives with no opportunity to escape.[14]

---

12. *A Friday Sermon on PA TV: ... We Must Educate our Children on the Love of Jihad...,* MEMRI (July 13, 2001), http://www.memri.org/report/en/0/0/0/0/0/0/478.htm.

13. *Friday Sermon on PA TV: Blessings to Whoever Saved a Bullet to Stick It In a Jew's Head,* MEMRI (Aug. 8, 2001), http://www.memri.org/report/en/0/0/0/0/0/0/492.htm.

14. *See* Kenneth R. Timmerman, Preachers of Hate: Islam and the War on America 156 (2003) (concerning subject matter taught in Islamic schools). "In third grade, children learn hate through vocabulary. 'The Zionist enemy attacked civilians with its aircraft.' (*Our Arabic Language for Third Grade,* part 2, #523, at 9) In sixth grade, hate became a drill. 'Who is the thief

The radical madrasas is like a conveyor belt of death where an unlimited number of suicide bombers emerge convinced that their religion demands the murder of Westerners, Jews, or anyone holding a contrary worldview.

As improbable as it sounds, the goal of radical Islam is to conquer the world. In 2006 alone, Ayman al-Zawahiri and Osama bin Laden made almost 20 videotaped pronouncements on the global war. Impressive then, but nothing compared with today's cyberspace superhighway (*see* Chapter 10 on ISIS). In August 2006, Zawahiri told his followers: "All the world is a battlefield open in front of us." This idea of global jihad is one of the defining threads that brings together militants and suicide murderers from Boston to Baghdad to Bali. In this light, the large active radical Islamic groups like ISIS and al-Qa'eda are both cohesive terror organizations and sources of inspiration for all like-minded fanatics.

Although radical Islam is not restricted to just the al-Qa'eda-styled belief system—the current Iranian theocratic regime has its own radicalized view of Islam—the modern roots of many of these groups stem from a Sunni strain of Islam known as the *Wahhabi* movement. The movement arose in the eighteenth century under Mohammed Ibn Abd al-Wahab in the desert of Najd in the Arabian Peninsula. Ibn Abd al-Wahab converted a group of illiterate Bedouins under Muhammad Ibn Sa'ud and declared himself the religious leader, or *Sheikh*, and Sa'ud the political leader, or *Emir*.

Amazingly, one of al-Wahab's first acts was to issue a *fatwa* (a religious decree), casting all non-Wahhabi Muslims as apostates and idol worshippers. In this way, Sa'ud's men were now all cloaked in the role of fighters for jihad against anyone not in the new Wahhabi movement, mostly including other Muslims whom they killed in large numbers.

---

who has torn our homeland?' (*Our Arabic Language for Sixth Grade*, part 1, #553, at 15) By seventh grade, students are expected to have internalized anti-Semitism so they can recite it on their own. 'Why do the Jews hate Muslim unity and want to cause division among them? Give an example of the evil attempts of the Jews, from events happening today.' (*Islamic Education for Seventh Grade*, #745, at 19) In ninth grade students are told, 'One must beware of Jews, for they are treacherous and disloyal.' (*Islamic Education for Ninth Grade*, #589, at 79)."

Funded in large part by the Kingdom of Saudi Arabia, the Wahhabi movement has spread across much of the Islamic world. In fact, their greatest achievement has been to present Wahhabism to a large segment of the Arab world as an accepted part of Islam, even as the correct Islam.

Radical Islam is truly an anachronistic mind set, in complete conflict with modern concepts of plurality, human rights, and democracy. Without question, the rich tradition of religious tolerance in America is the antithesis of radical Islam. In a federal terror trial in Michigan of a radical Islamist, *United States v. Koubriti*,[15] the Court wrote:

> Wahhabis, Takfiris, and Salafists.... These groups regard the Islam that most Muslims practice today as impure and polluted by idolatry and Western influence .... These radical fundamentalist-Islamic groups see the world divided in two spheres; that is, Dar-al-Islam (House of Islam or Islamic Zone), where peace reigns (Sallam), and the Dar-al-Harb (House of War or War Zone), which prevents a true Islamic state. The latter is viewed by these radical fundamentalist-Islamic groups to include all infidel areas that must ultimately be conquered. Global jihad is the constant effort to achieve this goal.[16]

Radical Islam is vastly different from all previous hate movements with which civilized nations have had to cope. Threatened by the values of democracy, freedom, and human rights, radical Islam is dedicated to the destruction of the West and all those who adopt Western ideals, including those moderate Muslim and Arab governments that refute their view of Islam. The religious based fanaticism runs so deep that they are eagerly willing to kill themselves in the furtherance of their cause. Unlike previous terrorist groups, Islamist suicide bombers have no "exit" strategy to save them-

---

15. *United States v. Koubriti*, 199 F. Supp. 2d 656 (E.D. Mich. S.D. 2002).
16. See Second Superseding Indictment, *U.S. v. Koubriti*, 199 F. Supp. 2d 656 (E.D. Mich. 2002) (No. 01-80778), *available at* http://fl1.findlaw.com/news.findlaw.com/hdocs/terrorism/uskoubriti82802ind.pdf.

selves, making it almost impossible for law enforcement to stop them when they act alone or in small groups. The jihadist wants to die, they embrace death.

Reading Radical Islam's Koran

Coming from the world's largest Muslim-majority nation, Indonesia, *The Illusion of an Islamic State* concedes that "radicals [Muslims] employ the same language as Muslims in general ... but in reality they understand these terms differently."[17] Of course, this is an understatement but when it comes to the rejection of radical Islam by the majority of Muslims, this is undeniably a good thing.

Those who assert that it is ridiculous to blame jihadi terrorism on the Koran invariably never address the verses in the Koran. Ignoring the Koran altogether, they instead argue by false analogy that the Bible also has violent verses. As one author put it: "Blaming terrorism on passages from the Qur'an would be like blaming the Crusades on passages from the New Testament."[18] As will be discussed later, this is a fallacious argument.

But the crux of the matter is this: It matters little whether the followers of radical Islam properly understand the dictates of Islam as President Obama, or you, or I, or various religious scholars define them; rather, it matters that they believe that *they* are acting on behalf of Allah. They sincerely believe that they are religious driven and can easily point to religious verse and line to support their propaganda.[19] So, while some exhibit frustration that all Islam does not understand what the Koran *really* means, in the main that argument misses a great deal of the point—people read it as they want to read it and no amount of historical or factual argument will sway them. Interestingly, of course, the Islamist has the high ground when it comes to being dedicated to the original intent of the text.

To illustrate this conundrum—that people perceive things as

---

17. THE ILLUSION OF AN ISLAMIC STATE 28 (H. E. KYAI HAJI ABDURRAHMAN, ed., 2011).
18. Fawaz A. Gerges, JOURNEY OF THE JIHADIST 11 (2006).
19. *See* John Sutherland, *The Middle East in Crisis*, ARMCHAIR GENERAL, March 2015, at 45.

they want to perceive them—I can point to direct statements in the Bible regarding the grace mechanics of salvation and yet many who claim that they are Christians reject the strict constructionist reading of salvation by faith alone in Christ alone and add in human merit and morality as additional requirements.

Although the grace system of belief revealed in Christianity is totally antithetical to the works formula for salvation found in all the other world religions, to include Islam, the concept of human morality and works as a vehicle to gain the approbation of God is a constant plague to Bible-based Christian doctrine. To be sure, Christians are commanded to follow the moral laws set out in the Bible, but this obligation is not a requirement for salvation. Salvation is appropriated freely based on a one-shot decision in a moment of time to believe in Christ. For example, when a Roman official asked what he had to do to be saved, Acts 16:31 records that Paul and Silas said: "Believe in the Lord Jesus Christ, and you shall be saved, and your house [should also do the same]."

Those "Christians" in opposition to salvation by grace simply believe things as they want to believe them, regardless of the scripture.[20] In his multi-volume work on systematic theology, Dr. Lewis Sperry Chafer, late president and professor of systematic theology at Dallas Theological Seminary, wrote:

> The idea that man will stand on a basis of personal worthiness has been the chief heresy, opposing the central doctrine of grace, from the time of Christ's death to the present hour. It so permeates the church that few who preach are able to exclude it from their attempts at gospel preaching. It is safe to say that wherever the element of human merit is allowed to intrude into the presentation of the plan of salvation, the message is satanic to that extent.[21]

20. *See* Thomas S. Kidd, *Who Is, Or Isn't Going to Hell?,'* USA TODAY, May 23, 2011, at A11 (discussing the fact that some Christians also unilaterally reject the Bible's clear and unequivocal statements about the existence of hell).
21. Lewis Sperry Chafer, 2 SYSTEMATIC THEOLOGY 110 (1947).

So too with reading Islam. Again, the debate about what the religion really says and the meaning that should be attached to what it says matters, but ultimately the only thing that matters is the number of Muslims that buy into the strict constructionist interpretation of Islam that leads directly to violent jihad.

So what does the Koran actually say? Many who read the Koran for the first time conclude that it is hopelessly convoluted due to the fact that it seemingly contains diametrically opposed passages. Some of the passages appear quite tolerant, reasonable, and peaceful while others are violent and hate filled. This duality is undeniable—there are surahs of peace and surahs of violence—but the apparent discrepancy can be reconciled by understanding the chronology of how the Koran was put together coupled with the concept of abrogation.

Remember, Muhammad could not read or write and issued a series of statements about what Allah revealed to him over a period of approximately 23 years. The earlier verses were spoken by Muhammad while he lived peacefully in the city of Mecca (from 610 to 622). There is no argument that these verses are replete with commands from Allah that embrace peace, friendship, charity, and religious tolerance with no instructions for Muslins to fight Jews, Christians, or anybody else.[22] Violence was neither preached nor advocated. In one often repeated Meccan hadith Muhammad said:

> Beware! Whoever is cruel and hard on a non-Muslim minority, or curtails their rights, or burdens them with more than they can bear, or takes anything from them against their free will, I will complain against that person on the Day of Judgment [as a works-religion Allah holds a judgment to determine admission to paradise].[23]

> [Muslims], argue only in the best way with the People of the Book [Jews and Christians], except with those of them

22. Mohamed Dajani, *Teaching Our Children Islam's True Message*, THE WASHINGTON INSTITUTE FOR NEAR EAST POLICY, April 9, 2015.
23. THE RELIGION OF ISLAM, www.islamreligion.com/articles/207/viewall/tolerance-of-prophet-towards-other-religions/ (last visited Aug. 19, 2015).

who act unjustly. Say [to them], 'We believe in what was revealed to us and in what was revealed to you; Our God and
your God are one [and the same]; we are devoted to Him.
Koran [Meccan] 29:46

There is no compulsion in religion. Koran [Meccan] 2:256

However, after Muhammad raised an effective combat force
and began his military battles with other tribes and his old home
town of Mecca the verses take a dramatic change with new commands to engage in violence, slavery, and to hold an intolerance for
all other religions. These later verses in the Koran were dictated by
Muhammad during a ten year period from outside of Mecca and are
called the Medinan verses (from 622 to 632).

Conversion to Islam is no longer solely by an appeal to the doctrines of the new religion as in the Meccan verses, but by "fighting"
the unbelievers in the name of Allah until they submit. Muhammad
turned from a humble preacher of the religion of Islam to a powerful military/civil/political dictator. For instance, the Koran states:

Fighting the Unbelievers:

Fight them until there is no more persecution, and worship is
devoted to Allah. If they cease hostilities [submit or convert
to Islam], there can be no further hostility, except towards
aggressors [the word here *az-zalimun* refers to polytheists
and wrongdoers]. Koran [Medinan] 2:193

[Muslims] fight them until there is no more persecution,
and worship is devoted to Allah alone . . . . Koran [Medi-
nan] 8:39

Prophet [Muhammad], work hard [jihad] against the disbelievers and the hypocrites, and be tough with them. Hell
is their final home – an evil destination. Koran [Medinan]
9:73

You who believe [Muslims], do not take not the Jews and the Christians as allies [friends]. Koran [Medinan] 5:51

Fight those People of the Book [Jews and Christians] who do not believe in God and the Last Day [the judgment seat of Allah], who do not forbid what God and His messenger have forbidden, who do not obey the rule of justice, until they pay the tax and agree to submit. Koran [Medinan] 9:29

Those who wage war against Allah and His messenger and strive to spread corruption in the land should be punished by death, crucifixion, the amputation of an alternate hand or foot, or banishment from the land. Koran [Medinan] 5:33

[W]herever you encounter the polytheists, kill them, seize them, besiege them, ambush them – but if they turn [to belief in Allah], maintain the prayer, and pay the prescribed alms, let them go on their way... Koran [Medinan] 9:5

You who believe [Muslims], fight the disbelievers near you and let them find you standing firm. Koran [Medinan] 9:123

The disbelievers [non-Muslims] should not think they have won – they cannot escape. Koran [Medinan] 8:59

Behead Unbelievers:

I shall put terror into the hearts of the disbelievers [non-Muslims]. Strike above their necks and strike their fingertips. Koran [Medinan] 8:12

When you meet the disbelievers in battle, strike them in the neck, and once they are defeated, bind any captives firmly – later you can release them by grace or by ransom." Koran [Medinan] 47:4

Killing Apostates from Islam:

They [non-Muslims] would dearly like you to reject faith, as
they themselves have done, to be like them. So do not take
them as allies until they migrate [to Medina and become
Muslims] for Allah's cause. If they [Muslims who leave Is-
lam] turn, then seize and kill them wherever you encounter
them. Koran [Medinan] 4:89

Sex Slavery:
[Muhammad had at least 11 wives, plus sex slave-girls taken in
battle]

You are forbidden to take as wives . . . women already married, other than your slaves: God has ordained all this for
you. Koran [Medinan] 4:23–24

Prophet, We have made lawful for you the wives . . . and
any [female] slaves God has assigned to you through war ...
concerning their wives and slave-girls .... Koran [Medinan]
33:50

[W]ho guard their chastity from all but their spouses or their
[female] slaves – there is no blame attached to [relations
with] these . . . ." Koran [Medinan] 70:29–30

The Law of Abrogation
Obviously, when someone talks about Islam as a religion of "peace,"
they are referring to the earlier Meccan verses and not the later Medinan verses. Not surprisingly, radical Islam embraces the Medinan
verses arguing that under the law of abrogation, the later verses
overrule any earlier Meccan verses when there is a contradiction
between the two. It is just that simple. Since the later verses are the
violent filled passages they are the ones that must be followed.

Abrogation is a term well known in the legal field. For instance,
suppose the Supreme Court rules in 1990 that the law pertaining

to negligence is X. Then, in 2016, the Supreme Court changes its mind and says that the law is now Y. What is the law? The Court's ruling of Y abrogates the earlier ruling of X. The law is now Y.

Abrogation also works in the Christian Bible, but for the Christian the end result is the exact opposite than in Islam. Biblical abrogation means that many of the harsher mandates in the Old Testament are abolished by the tolerant mandates in the New Testament. Many of the Divine mandates in the Mosaic Law given to the early Hebrew nation to regulate criminal law, warfare, rituals, and hygiene practices are abolished (1 *Corinthians* 10:31–33; *Acts* 11:1–18). The Old Testament tied the State and Church together (*Hosea*), the New Testament separates them. Christians are commanded to submit to the governing power of the secular State (*Romans* 13:1–4) and to "render to Caesar the things that are Caesar's and to God the things that are God's" (*Matthew* 22:15–22). The Old Testament authorized at times offensive religious based warfare (*Joshua*), the New Testament does not except in the case of self-defense. Most importantly, conversion is accomplished only by presentation of the gospel by peaceful means (*Acts* 1:8), never by force of arms.

Other concepts in the Old Testament are kept.[24] The golden rule of "love your neighbor as yourself" in *Leviticus* 19:18 is carried forward in the New Testament (*Matthew* 7:12) and expanded by "turn the other cheek" (*Luke* 6:29) in maintaining *agape* (impersonal love) for antagonistic people in the sphere of ones personal life (this does not speak to the legitimate use of physical violence in true self-defense).

Christ is also said to fulfill the Old Testament's Mosaic Law in thought and deed. In fact, all the Old Testament rituals were teaching tools about the person and work of the coming Messiah. The only Christian ritual in the Church age is the Lord's Supper which consists of eating unleavened bread and drinking unfermented grape juice in order to concentrate on the person (the bread represents His perfect humanity) and work (the wine represents His work on the Cross) of Jesus Christ.[25]

---

24. War and Peace in Jewish Traditions (Robert S. Hirt, ed., 2007).
25. *See* 1 *Corinthians* 11:23–26.

Ticket to Paradise

As one would expect, radical Islam wholly embraces jihad and the dying in jihad as a shahid as its primary virtue. For instance, the official motto of the Muslim Brotherhood states:

> Allah is our objective, the Prophet is our leader, the Koran is our law, *jihad* is our way, dying in the way of Allah is our highest hope.[26]

Radical Islam offers an added incentive that bypasses the works-religion system of main-stream Islam and asserts that those who die killing the enemy in jihad do not go before the Judgment Seat of Allah for evaluation on their worthiness to enter paradise. Instead, these martyrs who seek *amalyat-al-esteshhadia* (the mission with the intent of martyrdom) by-pass the judgment of Allah and automatically enter paradise to receive their eternal rewards (to include a large number of female virgins to satisfy their needs). In point of fact, martyrdom in jihad is the only absolute guarantee that Allah will place the Muslim in paradise.

> For sure, Allah has bought from the believers their lives and their property in exchange for Paradise. They kill in the way of Allah, so they kill and are killed …. And who fulfills the promise more than Allah [Allah will keep his word]? So take the good news about the bargain you have concluded with Him [i.e., you die in jihad and Allah will admit you to paradise]. This is the magnificent eternal happiness. Koran [Medinan] 9:111

At first blush this may look like a grace-system for salvation as previously discussed in Chapter 5 and will be set out again in Chapter 11, but it is not. The jihadist must kill himself, which is clearly the ultimate human *work*. For instance, Nidal Malik Hasan, the jihadi murderer in the 2009 terror attack in Texas, who was shot

---

26. Ayaan Hirsi Ali, *'The Quran Is Our Law; Jihad Is Our Way'*, THE WALL STREET JOURNAL, February 18, 2011 *available at* http://www.wsj.com/articles/ SB10001424052748704132204576136590964621006.

but survived is not automatically saved; Hasan may only expect to get extra "points" at Allah's Judgment Seat in terms of his intent to die in jihad. After all, at his trial Hasan proudly proclaimed that he was "defending other Muslims" and acting in the name of Allah.

Whatever else might be observed about jihadists, they are, as we say in the Army Special Forces, "hard core." When I was on active military service, I had no qualms about killing the enemy, if necessary, but I really never had a desire to die myself in the process. As much as I love my country, I looked forward to drinking a beer on "R&R" and fraternizing with members of the opposite sex (you have to be clear about this factor in today's military). These people *want* to die. They are not having a good day unless they do die.

Of course, the fact that the jihadist is willing to die for his belief does not mean that the belief is true, only that he believes it to be true. As strange as this might seem the phenomenon of dying for what is believed is not a novel idea. The pages of human history are filled with people who have willingly died for what they believe. In World War II hundreds of Japanese pilots consciously killed themselves in kamikaze attacks because of their belief in the divinity of the Emperor.

On the other hand, and this is an important distinction, no human will die for a lie, something that they factually know is absolutely not true.[27] This truism is one of the strongest proofs for the historical reality of the fact of the resurrection of Jesus Christ from the dead. Many of the eye-witnesses, to include ten of the miserable cowards called His disciples (John is the only one that died of old age), independently died horrible deaths by Romans, Jews, and others, because they would not recant that they had factually seen Him alive from the dead over a 40 day period on the earth before He ascended into heaven at the Mount of Olives, just outside of Jerusalem.[28]

---

27. *But see* Charles Dickens, THE TALE OF TWO CITIES (1859).
28. *See* C. S. Lewis, MERE CHRISTIANITY (1952).

Chapter 8

The Veil is Not the Suicide Belt

"[T]he veil is not the suicide belt."[1]

—Fareed Zakaria

If radical Islam is the true Islam, does it follow that the belief system of all other Muslims is incorrect? Logically it would seem that the one excludes the other. But with religion—any religion—*both* positions can be held.

Let me illustrate. I am a non-denominational Christian. For many years now, at the request of law students, I have been teaching a Bible class at the law school which meets five times a week. I am a strict constructionist of the Bible and under the orthodoxy of isagogics, exegesis, and categories, I teach the line-by-line original intent of the author.

I sometimes ask my class to imagine if they were to query a fellow Christian: "Do you love Jesus?" The answer given would be a resounding: "Yes. I love Jesus!"

But then if they were to ask this same person some follow up questions such as: (1) explain the significance of the Hypostatic Union of the God/man; (2) explain redemption and reconciliation;

---

1. Fareed Zakaria, *Learning to Live with Radical Islam*, NEWSWEEK, March 9, 2009, at 28.

(3) explain a Theophany; (3) explain the ministries of God the Holy Spirit regarding the humanity of Jesus; (4) explain eternal security; (5) explain the Righteousness of God in the context of His Justice; (6) explain the Old Sin Nature as it applied to the impeccable nature of Christ; (7) explain the doctrine of Divine Decrees; (8) explain what happened on the Cross during the final three hours when Jesus screamed out, "My God, My God why have you forsaken me?"; etc., what would be the response?

In over 95 percent of the time, the answers would most certainly be: (1) I don't know; (2) I don't know; (3) I don't know; (4) I don't know; (5) I don't know; (6) I don't know; (7) I don't know; (8) I don't know; etc. ..., "But I love Jesus."

Clearly, one cannot love what one does not know. Still, most respondents would firmly adhere to the notion of being a "good" Christian.

The point is this. People can be totally ignorant of vast areas of their professed theology (in fact most are) and yet they are firmly convinced that this really doesn't matter as long as they strive to live a good moral lifestyle and are sincere about it. This same phenomenon is found in Islam, or for that matter in any religion. People simply know very little about their religion. Like most humans who claim identification to any given religion, the vast majority of Muslims are Muslims simply due to the fact that they were born into a Muslim family. Consequently, the only reason Islam is the fastest growing religion in the world is because Muslim families are large.

Daniel Akbari, a top Iranian lawyer and legal scholar of Islam, correctly observes that "many Muslims believe they are qualified to speak about Islam simply because they call themselves Muslim, even if they have not read the Koran, or, incredibly, even if they disagree with it."[2] They are not strict constructionists of the Koran, nor do they care to be. Indeed, most have no idea what Muslim theology is all about beyond a few of the good Meccan verses. For many followers of Islam, it means living a good moral life with the idea that if you are right with your fellow man, then you will be right with God.

2.   Daniel Akbari & Paul Tetreault, HONOR KILLING 9 (2014).

As previously discussed, the fact that some people have strongly held beliefs does not mean that those beliefs reflect actual truth,
only that they believe them to be true. On the other hand, there is
the person that reads and knows the dictates of the particular religious faith, but chooses to reject them in favor of some substitute
concept. These substitute concepts range from the man-made traditions that accompany the religion to their own personal set of norms
and standards.

For example, Thomas Jefferson wrote what is called the "Jefferson Bible."[3] Fancying himself a great thinker about God and
man, Jefferson took out his intellectually sharpened scissors and
cut out all the passages in the New Testament that did not comport
with his idea of what God should be like. If the verse offended his
personal *weltanschauung* (world view) he simply discarded it. Jefferson would be a "Christian," but only under his own theology.

Consciously or not, most humans do the same. They simply
ignore the parts they don't like or understand and adopt the parts
they do like. If this practice conflicts with the actual original meaning of the religious text, they ignore the original text or "interpret"
it to mean what they want it to mean. Those familiar with the history of the Catholic Church know that the Reformation started because certain Catholic priests such as Martin Luther rejected Catholic Church teachings and traditions of their day protesting that the
Church dramatically contradicted the plain wording of the Bible,
particularly over the issue of salvation by grace. They were called
the protestors, later the movement led to the Protestant denomina-
tion.

So, radical Islam may claim that they are the supreme strict
constructionists of the religion of Islam, but the majority of Muslims simply refuse to follow suit.[4] Radical Islam is an ultra-funda-
mentalist view of Islam that not only far surpasses moderate Muslims in their theology, it even goes far beyond those many millions

---

3.   Thomas Jefferson, JEFFERSON BIBLE (1895).
4.   Loren Thompson, *Five Reasons The ISIS Fight Isn't About Islam*, FORBES,
February 26, 2015 *available at* http://www.forbes.com/sites/lorenthomp-
son/2015/02/26/five-reasons-the-isis-fight-isnt-about-islam/.

of Muslims who willingly embrace things that are the antithesis of Western values such as Sharia courts, lack of religious freedom, and discrimination against women.

Thus, in discussing the reality of radical Islam it is important to realize that "the veil is not the suicide belt."[5] Muslims who follow even the most strict form of Sharia Law are not *ipso facto* going to murder. They follow the Jeffersonian approach to religion. Nevertheless, while not all fundamentalists of Islam are jihadists, all jihadists are ultra-fundamentalists.

Accordingly, it is vitally important to distinguish between radical Islam and all the rest of Islam, whether one labels all the rest of Islam as *fundamentalist* Islam; *moderate* Islam; or *modernized* Islam. The majority of the Muslim world does not embrace death in terrorism—*jihad*—as its highest virtue.

Integration in the West

As will be discussed later, the appeal of radical Islam resonates across broad categories of the social strata—rich and poor, educated and uneducated—but of great concern to Western countries is the fact that many Muslim immigrants to the West increasingly refuse to integrate into the culture and customs of their new country. Even those who benefit greatly from the prosperity of the West in terms of free market enterprise and education, still cling to fundamentalist Islam or radical Islam. The perpetrators of the terror attacks in Paris, London, Stockholm, Madrid, Boston, Brussels, New York, Toronto, Copenhagen, Sydney, etc., were Muslims who lived in those nations, many of them second generation Muslims.

The European Union is home or host to some 40.5 million legally established international migrants, representing about 8.3 percent of its total population. Of them some 27.3 million (5.6 percent of total population) have come from third world countries.[6] Many are Muslims.

---

5.   Fareed Zakaria, *Learning to Live with Radical Islam*, NEWSWEEK, March 9, 2009, at 28.
6.   Rainer Münz, Thomas Straubhaar, Florin Vadean, Nadia Vadean. "What are the migrants' contributions to employment and Growth? A European Approach" *Migration Research Group*. http://www.oecd.org/dev/38295272. pdf, January 2007.

Beyond the employment and social welfare issues attendant to this massive migration, many Muslims and the large number of children born to them are not integrating into the culture of the host nation. France is a prime illustration. France's city suburbs called *banlieues defavorisees*, particularly around Paris, are becoming separate Islamic societies cut off from France. Muslim immigrants increasingly reject French values and identity. Right under the nose of the French people, Sharia Law is rapidly displacing French civil code law in the so-called Muslim "no-go" zones.

A recent one-year study, consisting of 2,200-pages entitled, *Banlieue de la République* (Suburbs of the Republic), centered on the four "i's"—"Islam, immigration, identity and insecurity,"[7] lamented this trend. The report mainly focused on the areas of *Clichy Sous Bois* and *Montfermeil*, two Muslim enclaves just north of Paris. With the largest population of Muslims in Europe, almost six million, the report suggests that France is on the verge of major social unrest because Muslims prefer an Islamic identity to a French identity. They do not identify themselves as French. While the report finds that poverty is a pressing matter (the unemployment rate for Muslim youth in the suburbs of Paris is around 43 percent), it notes the paradox that Muslims eagerly want the social welfare benefits that the State provides, but want to keep their Muslim identity under Sharia Law. The report closes with a warning voiced by many in Europe: France must find a way to re-integrate its Muslim suburbs into the national project.[8]

This assimilation will never take place for those Muslims who enter Europe for the express purpose of taking over Europe for Allah. They may not come to commit actual violent jihad but they come to Europe to conquer with their birthrate. The Koran is replete with verses that heap praise on those Muslims who immigrate to non-Muslim areas in order to help spread fundamentalist Islam. They do not come to enjoy the benefits of freedom for there "is

---

7.   Kern, Soren, *French Suburbs Becoming "Separate Islamic Societies,"* GATE-STONE INSTITUTE: INTERNATIONAL POLICY COUNCIL. *http://www.gatestoneinstitute. org/2487/french-suburbs-islamic-societies*, October 2011.
8.   *Id.*

nothing in the United States [or Europe] that they enjoy but the freedom to expand Islam."[9]

> Those who believed and emigrated [to Medina] and strug-
> gled for Allah's cause with their possessions and persons,
> and those who gave refuge and help .... they will have for-
> giveness and generous provision. Koran [Medinan] 8:72;
> 74

---

9. Daniel Akbari, New Jihadist & Islam 33 (2013).

Chapter 9

Al-Qa'eda

"The confrontation that Islam calls for with these godless and apostate regimes does not know Socratic debates, Platonic ideals nor Aristotelian diplomacy. But it knows the dialogue of bullets, the ideals of assassination, bombing, and destruction, and the diplomacy of the cannon and machine-gun."[1]

—Al-Qa'eda Training Manual

Al-Qa'eda is the most familiar manifestation of radical Islam and has until recently dominated the headlines. Osama bin Laden's brazen terror attack on America in 2001 marked the end of the post-Cold war era and the start of the era of radical Islam:

> [W]e calculated in advance the number of casualties from the enemy, who would be killed based on the position of the tower. We calculated that the floors that would be hit would be three or four floors. I was the most optimistic of them all . . . due to my experience in this field, I was thinking that the fire from the gas in the plane would melt the iron structure of the building and collapse the area where the plane

---

1. THE AL-QA'EDA MANUAL 8 (2002), *available at* http://www.usdoj.gov/ag/trainingmanual.htm.

hit and all the floors above it only. This is all that we had hoped for."[2]

Following the 2011 death of its founder Osama bin Laden, some commentators believed that the organization would fade away. It has not. Al-Qa'eda has reconstituted and splintered out with vibrant sub-groups to include al-Qa'eda in Iraq, al-Qa'eda in the Arabian Peninsula, and al-Qa'eda in the Lands of the Islamic Maghreb.
 Al-Qa'eda (the Base) is an umbrella organization founded in 1988 by a Saudi Arabian named Osama bin Laden. Osama bin Laden formed the group out of elements of the Maktab al-Khidamat, an organization founded by Osama bin Laden and Abdallah Azzam (a member of a group called the Palestinian Muslim Brotherhood) in the early 1980s to provide money, equipment, and manpower to the Afghan resistance against the Soviet Union's occupation of Afghanistan. With the withdrawal of the Soviets in 1989, bin Laden used al-Qa'eda in order to redirect his efforts to "attack the enemies of Islam all over the world" in order to establish a pan-Islamic caliphate through the Muslim world. The religious view advanced by al-Qa'eda is a fixed, comprehensive ideology that targets for death anyone that disagrees with its very narrow set of mandates.

From the early 1990s until the end of 2001, al-Qa'eda operated openly in the country of Afghanistan with the complete support of the Pashtun-dominated Taliban government. During the tenure of the Taliban regime, the relationship between the Taliban and the al-Qa'eda terrorist organization provided a seminal example of State-supported terrorism. In fact, under the Taliban, Afghanistan became a terror training ground for tens of thousands of Arab and non-Arab al-Qa'eda militants including Saudis, Kashmirs, Chechens, Uzbeks, Uighurs, and others (including a number of Americans). These training camps sent cells of well-trained terrorists into numerous countries where they were encouraged to recruit additional members and carry out terrorist attacks on command.

---

2. The Global War on Terrorism: The First 100 Days, U.S. Department of State, *available at* http://2001-2009.state.gov/s/ct/rls/wh/6947.htm.

While al-Qa'eda has tens of thousands of supporters and low-level operatives worldwide, only carefully selected Muslim males are offered full membership. These recruits must sign an oath of allegiance called a *bayat*, swearing to carry out the dictates of al-Qa'eda leaders on penalty of death. They are then indoctrinated and trained extensively in assassination, kidnapping, explosives, small arms, hijacking, and torture.

In 2004, Jordanian Abu Musab al-Zarqawi proclaimed his allegiance to Osama bin Laden and headed al-Qa'eda in Iraq. He specifically targeted apostate Muslims (Shia) and their houses of worship, killing them by the hundreds. The Bush surge of 2007-2008 decimated al-Qa'eda in Iraq, but Osama bin Laden was still able to hide out in plain sight in Pakistan for many years, until a bold U.S. Special Operations mission killed him at his hideout in 2011. He was immediately replaced with the new leader, Egyptian born former Muslim Brotherhood member, Dr. Ayman al-Zawahiri.

Even with Osama bin Laden gone, the "poster-child" for radical Islam is still the al-Qa'eda organization which combines all of the forms of State related terror identified in chapter 1. They were, at one time, State-sponsored by the Taliban government of Afghanistan and continue to be State-supported by a few radical regimes. They also qualify as a sub-State terrorist organization because they have infiltrated and established terrorist cells in various nations throughout the world to include Somalia, Yemen, Pakistan, and Mali.[3]

Furthermore, the virus of al-Qa'eda ideology also influences individual terrorism. Their ideology of hate and intolerance has reached the minds of individuals who, although not directly tied to the organization, choose to commit terrorist acts because they have adopted the general theme and goal of the al-Qa'eda mindset.

Some have described al-Qa'eda as an entirely new type of entity in the world—not just a terrorist group but a "virtual-State" that normal criminal law processes simply cannot curtail. The virtual-State description is fundamentally valid. The al-Qa'eda virtu-

---

3. *See* William L. Painter, *Selected Issues in Homeland Security Policy for the 114th Congress*, CONGRESSIONAL RESEARCH SERVICE 7–57, May 19, 2015.

al-State exhibits many of the characteristics of the classic nation-State, but is able to walk in and out of the shadows of international law because it has no fixed geographic boundaries. For instance, the al-Qa'eda virtual-State certainly has a political arm and media section that directs its policy, a military composed of thousands of devoted killers, a treasury that raises funds across the globe, a large number of supporters and adherents, direct and indirect links to the leaders of other nation-states, etc.

For this reason, the United States has been obliged to reach beyond the tools of normal domestic law enforcement and utilize its military power to make war with this virtual-State. The war continues and al-Qa'eda central still thinks big. They still desire to attack America with the most destructive weapons that they can lay their hands on. The failed al-Qa'eda plot to detonate liquid explosives on as many as ten U.S. bound airplanes coming from London in August 2006 was their latest grand attempt. They will come again with another catastrophic strike. Unlike ISIS, who is focused for now at expanding the caliphate in the Middle East, al-Qa'eda is fixated almost entirely on attacking the United States again.

Chapter 10

ISIS & the Caliphate

"We will conquer Rome, by the will of Allah."[1]

—ISIS Lieutenant

Ad-Dawlah al-Islāmiyah fīl-'Irāq wash-Shām is known in the English-speaking world as the Islamic State of Iraq and the Levant (ISIL), later called the Islamic State of Iraq and al-Sham (ISIS). Although President Obama always used the old phrase of ISIL, the term the group prefers for itself is the Arabic word *ad-Dawlah* which means Islamic State (IS). The most common name for the group, however, is ISIS and the one used here.

ISIS is today's primary spearhead for radical Islam. "Following *takfiri* doctrine [proclaiming people to be apostates because of their sins] the Islamic State is committed to purifying the world by killing vast numbers of people."[2]

ISIS is a Sunni based radical Islamic terror group that originated as a sub-component of al-Qa'eda when Osama Bin Laden franchised his group into Iraq, following the toppling of the regime of Saddam Hussein in 2003 by the United States military. The near term goal of ISIS was to reestablish a single, transnational purely

---

1. David Von Drehle, *The European Front*, TIME, January 26, 2015 at 12.
2. Graeme Wood, *What ISIS Really Wants*, ATLANTIC, March 2015, at 82.

Islamic State based on Sharia Law—the next caliphate. The ruler of the caliphate is one supreme leader called the caliph. The caliph is akin to an absolute dictator who welds religious, military, and political power to govern an Islamic Sharia government with actual geographic dimensions.

ISIS formally established this caliphate in 2014 in parts of Syria and Iraq and has been expanding ever since. In the same way that Muhammad, Abu Bakr, and the other early leaders spread Islam, ISIS gives the new captured lands a choice, either convert to Islam or be killed (People of the Book may submit as second class citizens and pay a special tax).

If nothing else can be said about ISIS, it is undeniable that it believes itself to reflect the true Islam and that God has chosen it alone to spread Islam as intended. Furthermore, ISIS holds a religious "end-of-times" belief that it is destined to be a key agent of the coming apocalypse decreed by Allah. No other radical Islamic group, to include al-Qa'eda, has such a strong end of the world religious scenario. As one commentator correctly put it: "The Islamic State is no mere collection of psychopaths. It is a religious group with carefully considered beliefs, among them that it is a key agent of the coming apocalypse."[3]

The world first took notice of the group, then called al-Qa'eda in Iraq (AQI), in May of 2004 when a grainy, low-quality videotaped recording was released showing the hooded leader Abu Musab al-Zarqawi, decapitate American hostage Nicholas Berg with a large knife.[4] The beheading would become the first of many as the charismatic Zarqawi attracted more and more followers. Zarqawi was able to unite several different Sunni-based radical Islamic groups under the banner of the Mujahedeen Shura Council, citing the Koran as the justification for the agenda and actions of AQI.

In September of 2005, Zarqawi decided to expand the fight against the United States and its coalition partners and gain a greater level of Sunni support by declaring war on the "apostate" Shia

---

3. Id.
4. The Short Life of Abu Musab al-Zarqawi, http://www.theatlantic.com/magazine/archive/2006/07/the-short-violent-life-of-abu-musab-al-zarqawi/304983/.

majority of Iraq. Zarqawi's goal was to ignite a full scale sectarian war against the majority population of Iraqi Shia Muslims. Zarqawi's AQI gleefully murdered thousands of Shia civilians in terror attacks in their mosques, marketplaces, homes, and workplaces.

Although Zarqawi was killed by an American air strike in 2006, his successor, Abu Hamza al-Mujaher (also known as al-Masri) took additional steps to consolidate the movement and announced the creation of the Islamic State of Iraq (ISI). Mujaher installed Abu Omar al-Baghdadi as the new leader of ISI (not to be confused with the current leader of ISIS, Abu Bakr al-Baghdadi).

With the dramatic change in U.S. strategy under the Bush surge of 30,000 additional American combat troops sent to Iraq in 2007, ISI was thrown on its heels. Not only did the surge account for the deaths of tens of thousands of Iraqi militants and jihadists, it caused a *Sawha* (Sunni awakening) and brought a semblance of stability to Iraq and the fledging government in Baghdad. With the active co-operation of many local Sunnis, ISI was reduced to something that resembled more of a criminal gang than Allah's new movement.

By 2010, both Mujaher and Omar al-Baghdadi were killed by U.S. and Iraqi forces in the city of Tikrit. Although ISI had a new leader by the name of Abu Bakr al-Baghdadi, it was a political decision by President Barack Obama in late 2011, coupled with an all-out civil war in Syria, that catapulted the group to international prominence.

Before his departure from office, President Bush had negotiated a deal with the new Iraqi government for U.S. forces to remain in Iraq through 2011 when all parties understood that a new agreement on the basing of American forces would be hammered out by the United States and Iraq. The conventional wisdom by all the military hierarchy was that 20–30 thousand American military forces would need to remain in Iraq in order to ensure sufficient time for the nascent Iraqi government to stand on its own. Iraqi stability was close, but not yet a reality.

In the fall of 2011, the situation in Iraq was analogous to a football game; it was the fourth quarter of the game and we were two touchdowns ahead. In keeping with his long standing political promise to remove American troops from Iraq, President Obama flatly rejected the notion of a continuing American military presence. Obama pulled the team off the playing field. The result, of course, was predictable. The tremendous vacuum created by the withdrawal of all American military forces spelled disaster for Iraq. At best, Iraq would simply fragment along the fault lines of Sunni, Shia, and Kurd. At worst, radical Islam would fill the void and the world would have another failed State on its hands.

Designed as a form of plausible deniability for the disaster that would befall Iraq due to the Obama withdrawal, the official Obama Administration line was that then Secretary of State Hillary Clinton failed to secure a status of forces agreement (SOFA) with the Iraqi government that would have allowed for the continued stationing of American military forces in Iraq. Thus, the Obama Administration could disingenuously claim that America had no choice but to leave. When the SOFA "negotiations" stalled and then shut down in late 2011, the departure was swift and dramatic. By December 31, 2011, America and the stability won by eight years of American blood and treasure was gone. All hell broke loose.

With the absence of American forces, then Iraqi Prime Minister Nouri al-Maliki (a Shiite) chose to further alienate Sunni participation in power sharing and looked to Shia Iran as a close ally. The nearly-defunct ISI could now emerge as a champion of the Sunni Iraqis.

Coterminous with Obama's withdrawal, a bloody civil war was brewing to the north; Syria's dictator Bashar al-Assad had elected to fight rather than flee when confronted with nationwide protests over his continued rule. Inspired by the siren song of the Arab Spring multitudes of Syrians paraded in the streets to oust the dictator Assad. But Assad would not surrender power as Egypt's Hosni Mubarak had done in 2011, when the Egyptian people took to the streets in nation-wide demonstrations.

Like his father before him, Assad knew that only brutal dictators survive. Egypt's Mubarak was a dictator but not a brutal dictator like Syria's Assad. Assad had no qualms about turning his military might on his own people. In a bloody civil war that continues unabated, with several competing components to include Iranian backed Hezbollah supporting Assad (along with Russia), hundreds of thousands of civilians have already lost their lives.

ISIS rightly understood the implications of the unrest in Syria and seized the opportunity to expand its own agenda. ISIS saw how the Muslim Brotherhood's newly elected President Mohammad Morsi took power from Mubarak and bet that they could take over Assad's secular State in Syria as well. Baghdadi quickly took the initiative in 2011 and began to send his fighters from Iraq across the border into Syria to oppose Assad's military. Although Morsi and his Islamist allies were removed from power by an Egyptian military *coup d'état* in July 2013, the goal of an ISIS caliphate encompassing all of Syria and Iraq is just as vibrant as ever.

Al-Qa'eda central (located in Pakistan) also saw opportunity in Syria. To distinguish its jihadi fighters in Syria, in 2012 Zawahiri created a new splinter group called the Jabhat al-Nusra, also known as the al-Nusra Front. The al-Nusra Front quickly gained a reputation as ferocious and skilled fighters, raking up many tactical successes against Assad's forces.

ISIS's Baghdadi also stepped up his strategy. In order to take full advantage of the growing Sunni discontent in Iraq and the absolute chaos in Syria, Baghdadi consolidated his power base in a way that would be unmistakable to the region and to the world—he established the floor plan for an actual religious based Muslim caliphate that would be absolutely faithful to the tenants of radical Islam. In April 2013, Baghdadi renamed ISI which, as stated, is now ISIS or IS.

In the eyes of thousands of his followers, Baghdadi appeared as a great military and religious leader even superior to al-Qa'eda. Consequently, friction erupted between al-Qa'eda's al-Nusra Front and ISIS even to the point of outright shooting episodes. When Abu Khalid al-Suri, al-Qa'eda's mediator to ISIS was executed by Baghdadi in January 2014, al-Qa'eda central quickly renounced ties with ISIS. Although all three Sunni jihadi groups—al-Qa'eda, ISIS, and al-Nusra Front—share the same religious message of the absolute supremacy of radical Islam and many of their members pass between them, for now ISIS has supplanted al-Qa'eda and emerged as the dominant voice of Sunni radical Islam.

And so, on July 5, 2014, dressed in flowing black robes and a turban, Abu Bakr al-Baghdadi stepped onto the raised pulpit at the Grand Mosque of al-Nuri, in Mosul, Iraq and delivered a Ramadan sermon officially declaring himself to be Amir al-Mu'minin Caliph Ibrahim of the Islamic State, the caliph of the caliphate of the new Islamic State. With a ten million dollar bounty on his head, this rare public appearance was a clear call to all devout Muslims to flock to his caliphate. By declaring himself to be the sole living successor to the founder of Islam, Muhammad, he set himself up as the rightful ruler of all Muslims everywhere in the world and awakened large sections of Koranic beliefs that had lain dormant for many years.[5]

An audio recording of Caliph Baghdadi[6] announcing new expansion for the caliphate was posted online in November 2014, wherein he states:

Oh Muslims, we give you good news by announcing the expansion of the Islamic State to new lands … the lands of Al Haramayn [Saudi Arabia], Yemen, Egypt, Libya and Algeria.[7]

While the vast majority of Muslims around the world ignore Baghdadi and his caliphate, tens of thousands of Muslims have heeded the call with more each and every day springing to action. By now it's clear that the admonitions of this self-proclaimed caliph do not go unanswered as Muslim foreign fighters from around the world make their way (or attempt to make their way) to the caliphate.[8] Not only from Muslim countries, but they come from Britain, France, Belgium, Italy, Spain, Holland, Germany, Canada, Australia, the United States, and so on.

---

5. Graeme Wood, *What ISIS Really Wants*, ATLANTIC, March 2015, at 82.
6. The self-proclaimed caliph is #54 on Forbes list of The World's Most Powerful People of 2014. *See #54 Abu Bakr Al-Baghdadi*, FORBES, February 26, 2015.
7. *See* Fadel, Leila, *With Cash And Cachet, The Islamic State Expands Its Empire*, NATIONAL PUBLIC RADIO, November 18, 2014.
8. *See* Rebecca Kaplan, *ISIS Recruiting Teenagers: Why the Government Is Sounding the Alarm*, CBS NEWS, March 10, 2015.

Terror Tactics of ISIS

The horrific tactics of ISIS are well known and from a military perspective, the use and publication of such atrocities serve as a double-edged sword. On the one hand, they do instill terror and fear—causing entire Iraqi and Syrian military units to simply throw down their weapons and flee—but on the other hand they alienate large portions of the local Sunni population as well as stiffen the resolve of neighboring Sunni nations such as Jordan and Egypt to take action to oppose ISIS when they otherwise might have been content sit on the sidelines.

Here then is the dangerous fallacy of not understanding radical Islam, ISIS does not think like we would expect them to think. The use of terrorism not only by beheading boys as young as 15, but other atrocities committed as its *modus operandi* to include: mass public executions; crucifixion; women forced into sex slavery with some made to bear the children of ISIS fighters; public lashings and amputations, which fellow members of the community are forced to watch; stoning to death in the streets for various crimes; child training camps for terror; burning or drowning people alive; pillaging and rape are done because they believe that the Koran commands them to do so. They do these things because they believe it is their religious duty to expand the geographical dimensions of the caliphate and to usher in the final apocalyptic war which will see the ultimate triumph of Islam over the entire world. As such, ISIS has no concern or shame for its tactics of terror. In fact, they celebrate it.

They have zero regard for the March 2015 report on ISIS by the United Nations human rights office which concluded that ISIS had committed the same types of crimes that were the subject of the Nuremberg War Crimes Tribunals following World War II: war crimes, crimes against humanity, and genocide.[9] According to the *Report on the Protection of Civilians in Armed Conflict in Iraq*,

---

9. Report on the Protection of Civilians in armed Conflict in Iraq: 6 July-10 September 2014 (August 18, 2014), http://www.ohchr.org/Documents/Countries/IQ/UNAMI_OHCHR_POC_Report_FINAL_6July_10September2014.pdf.

at least 24,015 civilians were murdered or injured during the first eight months of 2014 with millions of people displaced from their homes and with minorities consisting of Yezidis, Christians, and Shiite Muslims, explicitly targeted by ISIS.

The UN report found that all people in the region were callously victimized to include children, pregnant women, persons with disabilities, and the elderly. The Report went on to say that not only were children used as suicide bombers, soldiers, and human shields but they were also murdered by way of crucifixion, beheading, and being buried alive. Young girls were also abducted and regularly sold as sex slaves.

The UN report is valid. Under radical Islam, minorities such as Yezidi men are considered non-believers and therefore must choose between converting to Islam or death. Yezidi women must convert and then "marry" ISIS jihadists, but the girls might be raped and then sold.

Because Christians are listed in the Koran as People of the Book, the men are forced to either convert, pay a *jizyah* (toleration tax), leave their homes, or die. Those that flee are stripped of their possessions and subjected to physical and sexual assault by ISIS guards as they cross checkpoints. ISIS either destroys all Christian churches and dwellings or turns them into Mosques or ISIS homes.

The immediate goal of ISIS is to expand the geographical boundaries of the new caliphate. The use of raw terror on civilians or military personnel is the hallmark of ISIS who will use their fighters to take over an area and then immediately force the remaining Muslim inhabitants to submit to the strictness interpretation of Sharia Law. The pattern for ISIS's conquest is illustrated by the capture of Mosul, Iraq's second largest city, with a population of over one million people.

On the night of June 9, 2014, ISIS began a coordinated military assault on Mosul, which is located 400 kilometers north of Baghdad. Within half a day of street fighting, ISIS seized control of Mosul's airport, all of its television stations, and the office of the governor. Over 1,000 Sunni prisoners were set free but 670 Shia Muslims prisoners were executed. By the next day, the Iraqi military's 2nd Division had fled to the south, many without firing a shot, abandoning huge stores of American supplied weapons, ammunition, uniforms, military vehicles of all sorts, and other supplies.[10]

To immediately establish its absolute rule over Mosul, a dozen Muslim Imams including Muhammad al-Mansuri, of the Grand Mosque of Mosul, were summarily executed for refusing to swear loyalty to ISIS. While a poll tax was imposed on the Assyrians, all Christians in Mosul were either crucified, beheaded, or driven out of the city with only the clothes on their backs.[11] For the first time in 1,700 years, there are no Christians in Mosul.

Again, all that ISIS does is justified from a strict constructionist reading of the Koran. This is not only associated with the mass murders of thousands, but also with such issues as sex slavery. The women kuffar (infidels) may be taken as concubines or sold into sex slavery. With the fall of Mosul, ISIS distributed pamphlets to the remaining inhabitants explaining the new rules of Sharia. One pamphlet was entitled: *Questions and Answers on Female Slaves and Their Freedom*, which approved ISIS fighters having sex with non-Muslim girls and women.[12] ISIS justified these acts by citing specific passages in the Koran and set the following rules in the pamphlet:

"If she was a virgin, he (the owner) can have intercourse with her immediately after the ownership is fulfilled."

"If she was not a virgin, her uterus must be purified (wait for her period to be sure she is not pregnant.)"

---

10. Suadad Al Salhy, *Sunni Militants Drive Iraqi Army Out of Mosul*, THE NEW YORK TIMES, June 10, 2014, *available at* http://www.nytimes.com/2014/06/11/world/middleeast/militants-in-mosul.html.
11. Alissa J. Rubin, *ISIS Forces Last Iraqi Christians to Flee Mosul*, THE NEW YORK TIMES, July 18, 2014, at A1.
12. Greg Botehlo, *ISIS: Enslaving, Having Sex with 'Unbelieving' Women, Girls is OK*, CNN, December 13, 2014, *available at* http://www.cnn.com/2014/12/12/world/meast/isis-justification-female-slaves/.

"Two men who co-own a captive can't both have sex with her and that a man can't have intercourse with his wife's slave."

"It is permissible to have intercourse with the female slave who hasn't reached puberty if she is fit for intercourse ... however, if she is not fit for intercourse, he (the owner) can only enjoy her without intercourse."

Coming as an amazement to the West, but as standard operating procedure for those who employ a strict interpretation of Islam, ISIS has reestablished a vast system of sexual slavery in the conquered areas of Iraq and Syria.[13] Following the example of what Muhammad himself did and citing passages in the Koran, ISIS authorizes the rape and buying and selling of *sabaya* (slave) girls and women that are polytheists like the Yezidi Arabs in particular, but now Jewish and Christian woman as well. In fact, reports surfaced in the summer of 2015 that ISIS's caliph Abu Bakr al-Baghdadi repeatedly raped American aid worker Kayla Mueller and made her his personal sex slave after "marrying her."[14] Kayla was killed in captivity in February 2015.

A new ISIS "34-page manual issued this summer [2015] by the terror group's Research and Fatwa Department" provides the details on the booming sex trade to include forms for buying and selling.[15] According to an investigative article in the *New York Times*, a total of 5,270 Yezidis women and girls were abducted in 2014. The article went on to report:

To handle them, the Islamic State has developed a detailed bureaucracy of sex slavery, including sales contracts notarized by the ISIS-run Islamic courts. And the practice has become an established recruiting tool to lure men from

---

13. Rukmini Calmachi, *ISIS Enshrines a Theology of Rape*, THE NEW YORK TIMES, August 13, 2015, at A1.
14. *Id.*
15. *Id.*

deeply conservative Muslim societies [under Sharia Law], where casual sex is taboo and dating is forbidden.[16]

The Administration of the Caliphate

While ISIS rejects all man-made geographic designations of sovereignty, ISIS has racked up an impressive amount of territory, mostly in Syria, Iraq, and Libya. ISIS divides its captured territory into provinces called a *wilayah*. Although each wilayah has its own ruler, Baghdadi remains firmly in power by means of a council of advisors. ISIS "vice police" impose the harshest interpretations of Islam requiring all men to grow beards and all women to wear the *hijab* (a veil that covers the female head and upper chest) or *niqah* (a type of clothing that covers the face as well as other parts of the female body). All manifestations of other religions or cultures are destroyed.

To sustain its expanding caliphate, ISIS obtains its revenue by a variety of methods to include seized property, bank robberies, donations, ransom payments, heavy taxes, and black market sales of oil and antiquities. In Iraq, ISIS now controls about 1/3 of all the wheat-producing areas in the country and enjoyed the benefits of a bumper crop in 2015.[17]

The largest source of revenue is by means of selling oil and natural gas produced from the captured energy facilities and oil fields. Bringing in up to three million dollars each day, tanker trucks full of smuggled oil sell to the highest bidder on the black market. Buyers for ISIS oil are reported to be in Turkey, the Kurdistan region of Iraq, and even the Assad regime in Syria.[18] Sales of up to 150,000 barrels of oil per day from its fields in Iraq and Syria make ISIS the richest radical Islamic group in history. A 2014 estimate of ISIS's

---

16. *Id.*
17. Matt Bradley, *Islamic State's Hold Squeezes Iraq Food Supply*, WALL STREET JOURNAL, July 13, 2015, at A12.
18. Howard J. Shatz, *To Defeat ISIS, Follow the Money*, RAND FOUNDATION, 2015.

net worth was $2 billion,[19] the number in 2016 is probably closer to $5 billion.

And then there is the paperwork. It is one thing to capture territory, it is quite another to run it. The ISIS fighters have to be supplied and operations funded, but the captured cities require even greater attention. Water, electricity, food, hospitals, law enforcement, manufacturing, and overall infrastructure maintenance which comes with governance requires money and administration. From most all accounts; ISIS is able to keep the streets clean and meet the basic necessities of life for the civilian population it rules over.[20]

To do all these things means not only money, but the efficient administration of money. Since ISIS operates primarily on a cash-basis system, money laundering activities are very active with much of the money transferred by means of couriers. From captured documents, it is well known that ISIS maintains meticulous payroll sheets and financial records. For instance, for its personnel, each member receives a flat monthly rate per person with an additional fixed amount for each wife, child, and dependent unmarried adult woman in each household (many are sex slaves). These types of payments will continue to the family even if the fighter is killed. Additional expenditures include rent for some members, bonuses, and medical expenses. ISIS also actively recruits the local youth, paying from $200 to $500 a month to young men.

Military Supplies

The main military arm of ISIS is loosely headquartered in the Raqqah area of Syria. While the majority of its fighters are Syrians, ISIS relies heavily on foreign fighters to supply its ever depleting rank and file, with almost half of the militants coming from outside Syria. Estimates of the total number of fighters vary, but as of 2016 a fair guess would now be around 70,000.[21]

19. Howard J. Shatz, *How ISIS Funds Its Reign of Terror*, RAND FOUNDATION, 2015.
20. Ammar Al Shamary & Gilgamesh Nabeel, *After a Year Under Islamic State, Mosul Now in "Dark Ages,"* USA TODAY, June 22, 2015, at 8A (setting out a detailed description of how ISIS rules the people in Mosul, Iraq).
21. Mary Ann Weaver, *Her Majesty's Jihadists*, NEW YORK TIMES, April 19, 2015, at MM42.

The Middle East is overflowing with weapons of every sort and ISIS has a full array of weapons and men that know how to use them. ISIS makes use of both the traditional weapons of terror such as car bombs, suicide bombers, and improvised explosive devices (IEDs) and the more advanced weaponry it has acquired by military conquest.

They are heavily armed, primarily from the contents of captured arsenals and battlefield pickups. For instance, after the capture of the Syrian 121st artillery regiment in 2014, ISIS captured: twelve 130mm M-46 towed field guns along with dozens of crates of ammunition; seven BM-21 truck-mounted multiple rocket launchers (MRLs); 400-500 accompanying 122mm Grad rockets; several Russian made T-55 main battle tanks; hundreds of rocket-propelled grenades (RPGs); tens of thousands of rounds of small-arms ammunition; dozens of military vehicles, hundreds of assault rifles and hand grenades; and several anti-tank guided missiles (ATGMs).[22]

ISIS and Social Media

As Chairman of the House Committee on Homeland Security Michael McCaul put it: "terrorism has gone viral."[23] One of the most surprising aspects of ISIS is its very successful use of cyberspace to get its message out, recruit, and fund the caliphate. The Internet is extremely prominent in today's world and ISIS has taken full advantage, using its younger Internet savvy members with great effect. Through social media and modern technology ISIS has been able to manipulate real or imagined grievances and successfully incite the younger generation of Muslims, especially Western Muslims, to join in their cause.[24]

Getting new members is vital to ISIS and recruitment of new members through a carefully coordinated social media campaign

22. Charles Lister, *Not Just Iraq, ISIS Also on the March in Syria*, Huffington Post, June 07, 2014.

23. Susan Page, *CIA Vet: War "Far As I Can See,"* USA Today, May 11, 2015, at A1.

24. *Youth Online and at Risk of Radicalization Facilitated by the Internet*, National Security Criminal Investigations Program of the Royal Canadian Mounted Police (June 7, 2011), http://www.rcmp-grc.gc.ca/nsci-ecsn/rad/youth-jeune-eng.pdf.

which operates over 50,000 social media accounts has borne much fruit. ISIS takes full advantage of cyberspace aiming their propaganda at young and in some cases economically challenged Muslims all over the globe who crave the attention and the feeling of belonging. The main demographic for recruitment is a young male adult, primarily in their late teens or early twenties, who are of Sunni Muslim decent. The Internet and social media are ISIS' modern vehicles for publicity and continuous communication. By means of social media such as Twitter, Facebook, Google, YouTube, WhatsApp, Skype, FaceTime, and Instagram, the message of jihad reaches farther than any previous terror group could have hoped to do.

This explosion of social media reflects not only the post-modernist emptiness of the masses as they wander mindlessly through time and space with nothing to say except to say, but also that some of these mindless stooges are fertile ground for a movement that provides a message of anti-establishment while offering a sense of belonging with the promise of Allah's blessing in eternity. It works. Younger Muslims from all over the world race to Iraq and Syria to join the Islamic State.[25]

ISIS has infiltrated blogs, like "Authentic Tauheed,"[26] created Applications, like "The Dawn of Glad Tidings," and infiltrated Twitter with thousands of accounts to promote the importance of its religious message, and to recruit.[27] Each social media platform controlled by ISIS is followed and observed by thousands and thousands of individuals in the West and in the Middle East.[28]

---

25. *How Terrorists Are Using Social Media: Terrorists Groups Are 'Embracing The Web' More Than Ever*, The Telegraph, November 4, 2014, *available at* http://www.telegraph.co.uk/news/worldnews/islamic-state/11207681/ How-terrorists-are-using-social-media.html.
26. *United States of America v. Rahatul Ashikim Khan, a/k/a, "Rahat Khan," a/k/a, "AutheticTauheed19," a/k/a, "AT19"*, No. A-14-M-285 (Western D. Texas filed June 17, 2014).
27. Doug Bernard, *ISIL Wages Skilled Social Media War*, Voice of America, June 18, 2014, http://www.voanews.com/content/isil-wages-skilled-social-media-war/1939505.html.
28. J.M. Berger, *How ISIS Games Twitter*, Atlantic, June 16, 2014, *available at* http://www.theatlantic.com/international/archive/2014/06/isis-iraq-twit-

ISIS also uses Facebook and other sites to solicit funding.[29] It was through Facebook, especially its messaging system, that ISIS was able to first begin soliciting funding online, and continues to do so.[30]

In terms of getting their message of radical Islam out, the Internet is priceless. When ISIS uploaded a video via YouTube showing the beheading of American journalist James Foley, it went viral. The video was extremely graphic, showing how the knife cut Foley's throat, and how the decapitated head was placed on top of the lifeless body. With the Internet as their world-wide press agency, ISIS is able to grab the world's attention in any manner they wish.

With new members that are trained in the fast moving world of cyber, ISIS has been very good at thwarting efforts to defeat them. While law enforcement is able to infiltrate ISIS blogs with undercover agents, they lack the ability to infiltrate private messaging through privately owned social media domains.[31] ISIS has also become stealth on social media sites.[32] They do not enable location features on their smartphones[33] and use different time zones, locations, and biographical fields avoiding the deciphering of their exact location on their social media.[34]

ISIS has learned quickly how to hide the locations of their posts on Twitter accounts and to not advertise any identifying information about themselves. In addition, they have learned to create min-

ter-social-media-strategy/372856/.

29. Brooke Satti, *Funding Terrorists: The Rise of ISIS*, SECURITY INTELLIGENCE, October 10, 2014, http://securityintelligence.com/funding-terrorists-the-rise-of-isis/#.VR9AN0KJndl.

30. Jacob Siegel, *ISIS is Using Social Media to Reach YOU, Its New Audience*, THE DAILY BEAST, August 31, 2014, http://www.thedailybeast.com/articles/2014/08/31/isis-s-use-of-social-media-to-reach-you-its-new-audience.html.

31. *United States of America v. Rahatul Ashikim Khan, a/k/a, "Rahat Khan," a/k/a, "AutheticTauheed19," a/k/a, "AT19"*, No. A-14-M-285 (Western D. Texas filed June 17, 2014).

32. J.M. Berger & Jonathon Morgan, *The ISIS Twitter Census: Defining and Describing the Population of ISIS Supporters on Twitter*, THE BROOKINGS PROJECT ON U.S. RELATIONS WITH THE ISLAMIC WORLD, March 2015, at 1–68.

33. *Id.* at 11.

34. *Id.* at 12.

imally followed, private accounts to send vital messages to other members who then mass circulate to thousands of accounts with thousands of followers.[35] In a recent survey, out of the 43,538 ISIS run Twitter accounts, only 3 percent had enabled the location feature on their smartphones, allowing their coordinates to be tracked. Shortly after it was discovered that some ISIS members had this feature enabled, top ISIS coordinators ordered members to disable the feature or have their phones destroyed.[36]

While the FBI and other federal agencies have implemented "an effective counter narrative" in the cyber world online, they admit that "the sheer volume" of ISIS messaging online, particularly through social media, "eclipses our effort."[37] ISIS is winning.

The European Front

With the 2015 ISIS terror attacks in Tunisia and Libya, ISIS central is on the doorstep of Europe. In 2015, ISIS released a video showing 21 Egyptian Christians as they were beheaded on the Libyan shoreline. The ISIS murderers then pointed across the Mediterranean and shouted: "We will conquer Rome, by the will of Allah."[38] This is the far term goal.

Once labeled as a junior varsity team by Barack Obama, ISIS has shown that it is most certainly not in the minor league, but rather a world class threat exploding across the Middle East in a blitzkrieg of brutality and violence which stretches from Syria, across Iraq and into Libya, Algeria, and other Middle Eastern nations. Even to the most uniformed member of our society, it should be clear that ISIS is not just another Islamic terror group of little significance as President Obama pronounced, it is on the move and growing in scope in two significant spheres.

---

35. J.M. Berger & Jonathon Morgan, *The ISIS Twitter Census: Defining and Describing the Population of ISIS Supporters on Twitter*, THE BROOKINGS PROJECT ON U.S. RELATIONS WITH THE ISLAMIC WORLD, March 2015, at 23.
36. *Id.*
37. Mike Levine, *FBI: "We Are Losing the Battle" to Stop ISIS Radicalization Online*, ABC NEWS, February 26, 2015, http://abcnews.go.com/News/fbi-losing-battle-stop-isis-radicalization-online/story?id=29241652.
38. David Von Drehle, *The European Front*, TIME, January 15, 2015 at 12.

First, it is gobbling up large areas of territory in the Middle East with absolutely no concern for the traditional demarcations of State borders or boundaries. This fact alone makes it a danger to American strategic interests in the region.

Second, ISIS serves as a pulsating ideological and religious beacon which inspires and energizes jihadists throughout the world to come off the sidelines and take physical action. It is a religious power source for a call to arms. Unlike its once sister organization al-Qa'eda which functions underground in the shadows of the nations that it operates from, ISIS boldly operates above the ground, heartedly waving the black flag of radical Islam for all the world to see. Touting its many lopsided military victories won on the battlefield against incredible odds, ISIS claims that it alone fulfills the religious narrative that is the touchstone for all true Muslims. It is the one and only caliphate.

In other words, from the perspective of the Islamist there is simply no reasonable expectation that ISIS should be able to defeat much bigger and much better supplied opponents... unless Allah was on their side. This narrative fits perfectly with the Battle of Badr in 624 when Muhammad's army, ill-trained and outnumbered, emerged victorious against its arch enemy in Mecca. Thus, if Allah is on their side then the caliphate is invincible and must be followed, since Allah cannot be defeated. More than any other factor, this overtly religious message is what excites the followers of radical Islam across world. No longer can the jihadist remain dormant in the domain of the impure, bastardized nations of the world. They must support the caliphate by actual violent jihad or provide material support so others can do actual violent jihad.

The willingness of European Muslims to surge to the Middle East to join ISIS has made ISIS more than just another terrorist group. As noted, the use of social media allows ISIS facilitators to privately message routes for new recruits to access ISIS in Syria with minimal, if any, insight or investigation by the government. The route takes the jihadist from Europe to Turkey and then across the border into Syria.[39] Once in Turkey, the ill-controlled border al-

---

39. Richard Engel, *Turkey, Syria Border Becoming Highway to Jihad*, NBC

lows easy access by foot or bus into Syria and territories controlled by ISIS.[40] "The number of Europeans joining Islamist fighters in Syria and Iraq has risen to more than 3,000, the EU's anti-terrorism chief told the BBC in 2014."[41] One of the more infamous Westerners to join ISIS is Mohammed Emwazi, known as Jihadi John. Leaving his home in England, Emwazi is well known for his appearances in ISIS videos where he is proudly seen beheading several victims in Syria.[42]

EUROPOL concluded that as of early 2015 approximately 5,000 citizens from different European countries had either made the trip to Syria to fight alongside ISIS, or they had received training of some sort, either online or in person and remained in the European Union.[43] Other figures by European intelligence services show that a minimum of 480 or 20 percent of the 2,400 suspected European citizens who have traveled to Syria to become part of ISIS had died in training or fighting.[44]

Clearly, most Western Muslim recruits never return from the frontlines of ISIS, but some do. Many Muslims in Europe possess Western passports which allow them to enter and exit at their leisure. This also means that ISIS can train European Muslims and then send them back to do jihad in Europe.[45] Coupled with those jihadists that remain at home but are influenced by ISIS, the threat

---

NEWS, February 25, 2015, http://www.nbcnews.com/nightly-news/video/turkey--syria-border-becoming-highway-to-jihad-404464707686.

40. Jacob Siegel, *ISIS is Using Social Media to Reach YOU, Its New Audience*, THE DAILY BEAST, August 31, 2014, http://www.thedailybeast.com/articles/2014/08/31/isis-s-use-of-social-media-to-reach-you-its-new-audience.html.

41. *Islamic State Crisis: 3,000 European Jihadists Join Fight*, THE BBC, September 13, 2014, http://www.bbc.com/news/world-middle-east-29372494.

42. John Bacon, *Man Known as 'Jihadi John' Once Considered Suicide*, USA TODAY, March 1, 2015, at A1.

43. Charlotte McDonald-Gibson, *How ISIS Threatens Europe*, TIME, February 26, 2015, http://time.com/3720076/isis-europe-migrants/.

44. Daniel Byman & Jeremy Shapiro, *Be Afraid. Be a Little Afraid: The Threat of Terrorism from Western Foreign Fighters in Syria and Iraq*, FOREIGN POLICY AT BROOKING, November 2014, at 1.

45. *Id.*

of ISIS is no longer something that is "over there." It is here in the West. The fear that these men will return home and either wage jihad against their home countries or will train others to do so is great. According to French officials, of the 930 known French citizens to have traveled to Syria to join the caliphate as of September 2014, 180 of them had returned to French soil.[46]

Due to the magnitude of Muslims from Europe going to train in Syria and then traveling back to Western soil, it was a statistical certainty that jihadist attacks within Europe would spike.[47] They did.

In 2014, Belgium experienced a terror attack from an ISIS fighter who had just returned from Syria. This radical Islamist targeted a Jewish museum in Brussels and shot to death four innocent people.

Immediately following the *Charlie Hebdo* attack in January 2015, a well-armed ISIS cell was broken up in Belgium. On the radar screen of Belgian security forces already, a safe house for a group of ISIS veterans was raided by Belgian police and military. What ensued was called "the largest firefight the Belgian commandos had faced since World War II."[48] Two ISIS members shot it out with automatic weapons and grenades and were killed.

In August 2015, Ayoub El-Khazzani, a "Moroccan with ties to radical Islam" attempted to conduct mass murder on a high-speed train from Amsterdam to Paris. Armed with a Kalashnikov and eight magazines of bullets he was subdued by three Americans who wrestled him to the ground and disarmed him.[49]

---

46. RFI, *930 French Residents Have Joined Jihadi Groups in Iraq and Syria, Minister*, RFI English, September 14, 2014, http://www.english.rfi.fr/france/20140914-930-french-residents-have-joined-jihadi-groups-iraq-and-syria-minister.

47. Daniel Byman & Jeremy Shapiro, *Be Afraid. Be a Little Afraid: The Threat of Terrorism from Western Foreign Fighters in Syria and Iraq*, FOREIGN POLICY AT BROOKING, November 2014, at 1.

48. *See* Paul Cruickshank, *Inside ISIS Plot to Attack the Heart of Europe*, CNN, February 13, 2015.

49. John Bacon, *Train Heroes Acted on Instinct*, USA TODAY, August 24, 2015, at A1.

Some Muslim females also support ISIS. The February 2015 case of three 15 and 16 year old Muslim girls traveling from London to Turkey to become jihadi wives in Syria, is only one example that received much media attention due to the tender ages of the girls. Following the encouragement and radicalization by a school friend who had traveled to Syria two months prior with the same objective, these girls willingly sought to enter the ranks of radical Islam.[50]

And of course there are the trademark terror murders of ISIS inspired attacks—beheadings. In September 2014, a London woman was attacked in her garden and beheaded by a Muslim convert named Nicolas Salvadore. In January 2015, Yassin Salhi cut off the head of Herve Cornara in Lyon, France. The radical Islamic fanatic covered Cornara's head in Arabic writing and attached it to a factory gate along with two ISIS flags. In August 2015, a radical Islamist cut the head off a Swedish woman at an IKEA store, although the Swedish police called it a "stabbing" so as not to offend Muslims. The list goes on and on.

Attacks in the United States

On May 3, 2015, two radical Muslim male jihadists clad in body armor and carrying semi-automatic weapons were killed in a shootout with police as they attempted to conduct a mass casualty terror attack at a Muhammad Art Exhibit being held at the Curtis Culwell Center in Garland Texas (near Dallas, Texas). The two Muslim terrorists, Elton Simpson and Nadir Soofi, were roommates from Phoenix, Arizona, who had traveled across country to conduct the terror attack. Simpson, known as a jihadi sympathizer, had been convicted in federal court on terrorism related charges in 2011 for lying to federal investigators about his plan to travel to Somalia to engage in "violent jihad."[51]

---

50. *Families to Three Missing UK Girls Believed in Syria to Join ISIS: 'Please Come Home,'* FOX News, February 23, 2015, http://www.foxnews.com/world/2015/02/23/families-issue-emotional-appeals-to-3-missing-uk-girls-believed-in-syria-to/.

51. Donna Leinwand Leger & William M. Welch, *Texas Shooting Suspect Had Ties to Islamic Jihad*, USA Today, May 5, 2015, at A1.

With the known influence of ISIS on America's radical Muslims, and with Simpson's connection to jihad in mind, on May 5, 2015, *USA Today* ran a front page article entitled: "Texas Shooting Suspect Had Ties to Islamic Jihad,"[52] where the paper pointed out that Simpson was a radical Islamist. The immediate question was the role that ISIS central played in the attack. Were these two only influenced by ISIS or were they actually command directed by ISIS? On May 6, 2015, the *Washington Post* ran a front page story entitled: "No Signs Islamic State Led Texas Plot,"[53] but the *Wall Street Journal* of May 6, 2015, acknowledged that the Islamic State had claimed responsibility for the attack through its radio station in Iraq.[54] ISIS proudly claimed that "two soldiers of the caliphate" had carried out the attack and warned that more were coming.

But is ISIS central really able to direct operations here in the United States? Or is it only that ISIS simply serves as an inspiration for domestic jihadists?

In the wake of the Garland attack, FBI Director James Comey told *ABC* news in an interview that there are "thousands" of followers of ISIS inside the United States[55] and that the number of American Muslims going to join ISIS is increasing at a rapid pace.[56] Comey's warnings are not news to anyone with a knowledge of radical Islam, what is disconcerting is that little is being done to stop them. Likewise, ISIS is able to inspire radicalized Muslims in America who are frustrated by an inability to leave the United States or just can't afford it, so they elect to commit jihad here in America.

Illustrations of ISIS inspired Americans to: (1) either stay here in America and kill for ISIS; (2) join ISIS and fight abroad; or (3) join

---

52. *Id.*

53. Sari Horwitz & Adam Goldman, *No Signs Islamic State Led Plot in Texas*, WASHINGTON POST, May 6, 2015, at A1.

54. Karen Leigh & David Barrett, *Probe of Gunman Wasn't Seen As Pressing*, WALL STREET JOURNAL, May 6, 2015, at A6.

55. Maggie Ybarra, *Islamic State Could Soon Execute 9/11 – Scale Attack in US*, WASHINGTON TIMES, May 8, 2015, at A1.

56. Sari Horwitz & Adam Goldman, *FBI Director: Number of Americans to fight in Syria Increasing*, WASHINGTON POST, May 2, 2014, at A1.

ISIS and then return to kill here in America, are too numerous to list and the numbers in each of the three categories increase each month. The influence of ISIS to inspire radical Islamists is skyrocketing in the United States to the point that the FBI now refers to the scores and scores of new arrests, that really began in earnest in the 2014–2015 time frame, as the "new normal" for the nation.

The Garland case represents the first category, where the two radical Muslims were inspired by ISIS to conduct jihad murder here in America. Attacks by radical Muslims prior to 2014 were not inspired by ISIS, but rather by other brands of radical Islam. Examples would include the Fort Hood terror attack in 2009 and the Boston Marathon bombings in April 2013, where two radical Muslims set off two bombs that killed three people and injured 264 others at a marathon race in Boston.

In September 2014, Oklahoma experienced an ISIS inspired jihad attack when Jah'Keem Yisrael, a convert to Islam who became radicalized while serving a prison term, cut off the head of a fellow worker at their worksite and was in the act of beheading a second woman when he was shot. Also in October 2014, a Muslim convert jihadist by the name of Zale Thompson was shot dead after he attacked a group of New York police officers with a large hatchet to decapitate them.

A week after Americans celebrated July 4, 2015, the Declaration of Independence holiday, the FBI Director revealed to the public that federal authorities had disrupted an undisclosed number of suspected radical Islamic terror plots set to "kill people in the United States"[57] over the holiday period. Then, a week later, Mohammod Youssef Abdulazeez, a Muslim born in Kuwait but raised in America, murdered four Marines and a Navy petty officer in a terror attack on military offices in Tennessee.[58] Abdulazeez had made recent trips to Jordan and Yemen but it is unknown how he became radicalized. Three days before the terror attacks, Abdulazeez posted

57. Kevin Johnson, *Feds Foil July 4 Terror Plots*, USA TODAY, July 10-12, 2015, at A1.
58. Matt Slovin & Doug Stanglin, *Four Marines Slain in Tennessee Shooting*, USA TODAY, July 17-19, 2015, at A1.

online that "life is short and bitter" and that Muslims should not let "the opportunity to submit to Allah … pass you by."[59] He was killed by police in a subsequent shoot-out.

In July 2015, Almlak Benitez, a Muslim convert, was charged with attempting to use a backpack bomb in a terror attack on a Florida beach in Key West, Florida, to show solidarity with ISIS. He posted on his Facebook that he was an "ISIS Muslim."

As in Europe, the second category speaks to those that desire to leave the United States and travel to Syria to in the United States join ISIS's caliphate and fight jihad there.[60] That number also grows by leaps and bounds each month. FBI Director Comey stated in 2014 that it was known that dozens of Americans were fighting with ISIS in Syria, estimating there may be more but it was difficult to predict the exact amount. A senior U.S. counterterrorism official expanded on Comey's statement, stating that within the first five months of 2014 alone, it was known that 60 Americans had traveled to join the Muslim caliphate in Syria.

The case of Tairod Nathan Webster Pugh, a U.S. Air Force veteran and onetime resident of San Antonio, Texas, represents the case of a convert to radical Islam attempting to join ISIS. After moving to San Antonio in 1998, he converted to Islam and became radical in his beliefs as seen through his social media accounts and discussions with friends of his support for Osama bin Laden. Pugh was arrested in March 2015 by the FBI and charged with a variety of crimes to include providing material support to ISIS.[61] Pugh had been fired from his job as an airplane mechanic in Kuwait and attempted to make the journey to join ISIS fighters in Syria before he was stopped and arrested.[62]

---

59. *Id.*

60. Other Americans have left the United States to join other radical Islamic groups, like the case of Ibrahim Abdurahman Mohamed, from Minnesota. Mohamed was killed leading the deadly assault on the Somali Parliament in Mogadishu in 2014, which left more than ten people dead.

61. Pierre Thomas, Mike Levine & Jack Cloherty, *Tairod Nathan Webster Pugh: Former US Air Force Mechanic Charged with Trying to Join ISIS in Syria*, ABC News, Mar. 17, 2015, http://abcnews.go.com/International/us-air-force-mechanic-charged-join-isis-syria/story?id=29699712.

62. *Id.*

In late 2014, ISIS utilized social media to persuade three Muslim females (referred to in the media as "jihadi Janes") from Colorado, to become more devout Muslims by "rejecting Western ways" and joining the fight for their religion in Syria.[63] ISIS sent the three radical Muslim girls detailed maps and plans on how to travel from Denver, Colorado to Syria by way of Turkey. They were arrested in Germany en route to Turkey.

In May 2015, six Somali-Americans ranging in age from 19-21 were charged with conspiring to join ISIS. Two were arrested in San Diego, California, going to Syria through Mexico.[64]

In July 2015, Arafat M. Nagi, of Lackawanna, New York, was arrested and charged with attempting to provide material support to ISIS. Nagi pledged allegiance to ISIS and had traveled twice to Turkey in 2012 and 2014 with the intent to return soon to join ISIS.

While one could go on and on, the discussion of this category of jihadist will conclude with a sampling of just the first two weeks in one month—August of 2015. In the first two weeks of August 2015 alone, the following eight jihadists were either arrested, charged, or convicted in the United States for attempting to travel to join ISIS or a sister radical Islamic terror group overseas: (1) Abdurasul Hasanovich Juraboev was convicted in New York federal court for attempting to travel to join ISIS. Juraboev also indicated that if unable to travel, he would kill here in the United States on command from ISIS to include killing President Obama or setting off a bomb in New York; (2) Argon Hasbajrami, a resident of New York, was sentenced to 16 years in federal prison for attempting to travel to Turkey with the intent to join radical Islamic terror groups in Afghanistan or Pakistan; (3) Lawal Olaniyi Babafemi was sentenced to 16 years in federal prison in New York for conspiring to provide material support to al-Qa'eda in the Arabian Peninsula; (4) Munther Omar Saleh, of Queens, New York, was charged in federal

---

63. Evan Perez, *Officials: U.S. Wants to Know How ISIS Recruited 3 Denver Teens*, CNN, November 13, 2014, http://www.cnn.com/2014/11/12/us/isis-teen-recruitment/.

64. Miriam Jordan, *From Students to Suspects*, WALL STREET JOURNAL, May 13, 2014, at A3.

court with providing material support to terrorism by attempting to travel to Syria to join ISIS; (5) Fareed Mumuni, of Staten Island, New York, was charged in federal court with providing material support to terrorism by attempting to travel to Syria to join ISIS; (6) Jaelyn Delshaun Young, of Mississippi, was arrested and charged with conspiring and attempting to provide material support to ISIS, the arrest was made at the airport in Columbus, Mississippi; (7) Muhammad Oda Dakhlalla was arrested and charged with providing material support to ISIS by attempting to travel overseas to join ISIS; and (8) Adam Dandach of Orange, California, was convicted in federal court for attempting to travel to Syria in order to join ISIS.

The third category, where Americans leave the U.S. to go to join ISIS and return to kill is of great concern to the FBI. These individuals receive professional solider skills from ISIS which they can then use to engage in more sophisticated terror attacks when they return to America. They come from ISIS central to the United States.

Eric Harroun, a former Army private (2000–2003), was an American Muslim convert who traveled to Syria and allegedly fought with the terror group al-Nusra Front. When he returned to the United States he was arrested and charged with various terror related offenses to include conspiracy to provide material support to a terrorist group. He was released after a secret plea deal with the federal government and died of a drug overdose in April 2014.

A more chilling case that represents this category is found in the 2014 arrest of an American Muslim college student from Texas. Rahatul Khan was charged with violating federal terrorism laws for his three-year involvement with recruiting and radicalizing Americans for ISIS to then conduct terrorism in America.[65] Khan joined an "internet-based chat room, 'Authentic Tauheed,'" in which he was recruited for jihad, and in turn recruited and radicalized other American Muslims. Khan connected his new recruits with fellow

---

65. *United States of America v. Rahatul Ashikim Khan, a/k/a, "Rahat Khan," a/k/a, "AutheticTauheed19," a/k/a, "AT19"*, No. A-14-M-285 (Western D. Texas filed June 17, 2014).

jihadists, providing them the same travel arrangements through Europe to Somalia or Syria to be trained and then to return to create the "third world war" on American soil.

ISIS has also motivated jihadists on America's immediate border in Canada (there are unconfirmed reports that ISIS may have cells in Mexico as well). ISIS claimed responsibility in the October 2014 shooting spree by Michael Zehaf-Bibeau, a convert to Islam, in Ottawa, Canada. One uniformed Canadian soldier was shot in the back and killed by Zehaf-Bibeau as he stood guard at Canada's National War Memorial. As Zehaf-Bibeau moved into the Canadian Parliament shooting his weapon to kill others, he was shot dead.

The Caliphate Will Attack America

In a front page story in the Washington Times on May 8, 2015, I was asked if ISIS was able to attack the United States in a similar manner as al-Qa'eda had done on 9/11.[66] I stated that "much Islamic State rhetoric may be bluster" but "if unchecked, it likely could execute a 9/11-scale attack in the U.S. a few years from now." Indeed, if they acquire a true WMD, we will wake to the news headline: "New York—Gone." Four days after my remarks, former CIA Director, Mike Morell agreed that it was "only a matter of time before the jihadist group [ISIS] is likely to be in a position to direct more elaborate attacks on American soil that could result in mass casualties."[67]

ISIS has inspired hundreds of Americans to act or attempt to act on their behalf, but these are the domestic jihadists not the jihadists operatives that would be sent into America from the ISIS caliphate, what I call ISIS central. The jihadists coming from ISIS central have the military skills and operational discipline to execute successful attacks, homegrown jihadists do not. Since 9/11 hundreds of terror attacks have been attempted here in the United States by homegrown jihadists that are inspired by radical Islam. In New

66. Maggie Ybarra, *Islamic State Could Soon Execute 9/11 – Scale Attack in US*, WASHINGTON TIMES, May 8, 2015, at A1.
67. Susan Page, *CIA Vet: War "Far As I Can See,"* USA TODAY, May 11, 2015, at A1.

York city alone, dozens of plots have been broken up by excellent law enforcement work at the State and federal level coupled with the fact that the vast majority have been unsuccessful because the operatives were sloppy and amateurish in either the planning or follow through.

ISIS central has the operational discipline required to strike us a heavy blow and cause fantastic mass casualties. It has the men, time, money, and skill to land a devastating terror attack on America, and they will do it. America may be war weary after the years in Afghanistan and Iraq, but fatigue has no counterpart with ISIS. ISIS is neglecting neither offensive nor defensive weapons and tactics.

In July 2015, the U.S. House of Representatives, Committee on Homeland Security (chaired by Congressman Mike McCall) issued a white paper entitled: *Terror Threat Snapshot*.[68] The paper listed three top takeaways:

(1) ISIS is dead set on attacking America and its allies. With the recent attacks in France and against tourists in Tunisia, ISIS has now been linked to 47 terrorist plots or attacks against the West, including 11 inside the United States. The rate of ISIS terror plots against the West has more than doubled in 2015 (19 plots in all of 2014; 28 already this year).

(2) The number of post-9/11 jihadi terror plots in the United States has surged. There have been more U.S.-based terror plots or attacks in the first half of 2015 (a total of 24) than in any full year since 9/11. Overall, homegrown jihadi plots have tripled in just the past five years (from 36 plots/attacks in June 2010 to 118 today).

(3) Islamist terrorists are getting better at recruiting Americans. Ten U.S.-based ISIS supporters have been arrested in the last month, bringing the total to 55 ISIS-inspired individuals arrested and charged in America (not included two which have been charged in absentia). ISIS followers have now been arrested in at least 19 States.

---

68. Terror Threat Snapshot, Committee on Homeland Security, July 2015.

ISIS probably can't carry out large-scale attacks in the U.S. right now, but such limitations can easily disappear. The Islamic State is certainly working on gaining that capability and it has a proven track record. It cost al-Qa'eda just under one million dollars to fund all of the logistics connected with the terror operation on 9/11. "ISIS has billions of dollars—with a 'b'—and if they plan an attack from over there, it's going to be 75 percent [probability] successful and larger than 9/11."[69]

Current Steps to Stop ISIS

In accordance with the historically documented reaction of most democracies to initially meet aggression with appeasement, our current policies are actually fostering the growth of ISIS. Both the United States and the international community are frozen in inaction, like deer in the headlights.

The international community has done little by way of concrete steps to blunt ISIS. In August 2015, the United Nations Security Council which is charged by the UN Charter with overseeing peace and stability in the world adopted Resolution 2170, which condemned the abuse of human rights by ISIS. The Security Council resolution strongly condemned the acts of kidnapping, execution, violence, and extrajudicial killings. It also strongly condemned the displacement of minority groups, killing and maiming of children, recruitment and use of children, rape and other forms of sexual violence, along with other acts of terror committed by ISIS.[70]

The UN Resolution is all very well and good but purely symbolic.[71] What is needed is a military estimate of the situation. Furthermore, given the track record of the international community, if the United States does not lead the way, nothing will be done to

---

69. Maggie Ybarra, *Islamic State Could Soon Execute 9/11 – Scale Attack in US*, WASHINGTON TIMES, May 8, 2015, at A1.

70. UNITED NATIONS SECURITY COUNCIL RESOLUTION 2170 (2014).

71. *Democracy's Decline: Crying for Freedom*, ECONOMIST (Jan. 14, 2010), http://www.economist.com/node/15270960 (According to the lobby group Freedom House, the number of electoral democracies in the world stands at 116 out of the 192 [there are now 193 members] nations in the United Nations).

stop the caliphate. President Obama correctly stated that: "If left unchecked, ISIL [sic] will pose a threat beyond the Middle East, including ... the United States homeland."[72]

So what is America doing about ISIS central? Is it working? Although the President already possesses the power under Article II of the US Constitution and the 2001 Congressional AUMF to direct the might of our military to obliterate ISIS, he refused to do so. Instead Obama elected to *appear* that he was doing something while in reality he did nothing of real substance. Obama did join a "coalition" of 40 nations that is content to drop a few bombs from the air here and there on ISIS targets in Iraq and sometimes in Syria. Obama also went to the Republican Congress with a ridiculous request to "tie my hands" in fighting ISIS.

On February 11, 2015, President Obama formally asked Congress to authorize the use of military force against ISIS, but only in a manner that would limit his application of such military force. President Obama's request to Congress to approve his Authorization of Use of Military Force (AUMF) against ISIS even contained a lapse period that would kick in after three years. In describing the logic of this proposal to Congress President Obama said:

> The authorization I propose would provide the flexibility to conduct ground combat operations in other, more limited circumstances, such as rescue operations involving U.S. or coalition personnel or the use of special operations forces to take military action against ISIL leadership .... It would also authorize the use of U.S. forces in situations where ground combat operations are not expected or intended, such as intelligence collection and sharing, missions to enable kinetic strikes, or the provision of operational planning and other forms of advice and assistance to partner forces.[73]

---

72. *Obama Opens Door to 'Limited' Ground Combat Operations Against ISIS*, FOX NEWS, February 11, 2015, http://www.foxnews.com/politics/2015/02/11/obama-proposes-war-authorization-against-islamic-state.
73. *Id.*

The Congress rightly never responded, in part because they smelled a political trap. If they had authorized a limited use of force as Obama insisted and ISIS later conducted a massive terror attack then they would have been blamed along with President Obama and the Democratic party for doing too little. In addition, they knew that Obama had already signaled his absolute refusal to use American ground forces against ISIS. So why bother?

For now "Operation Inherent Resolve," a coalition air campaign led by the United States, is coupled with gradual increases in the number of American "trainers" to assist the Iraqi military in terms of training and logistics, but not actual ground combat.[74] Apart from eliminating a few senior ISIS leaders, which are quickly replaced, the tally of success from the air strikes are minimal. An early assessment in 2015, boasted of destroying 77 tanks, 287 military vehicles, 416 staging areas, 1,757 buildings, 1,330 fighting positions, 152 pieces of oil infrastructure, and 2,078 oil targets.[75] One thing is clear, the bombing has not stopped the advance of ISIS to any great degree. They are winning.[76]

---

74. Kim Hjelmgaard & Jim Michaels, *Obama Vows to Bolster Iraqis,* USA TODAY, June 6, 2015, at A1.
75. Operation Inherent Resolve: Targeted Operations Against ISIL Terrorists, U.S. Department of Defense.
76. Jim Michaels, *Iraq Set to Retake Ramadi from ISIL,* USA TODAY, August 12, 2015, at A1.

Chapter 11

Short Term Solutions

"Speak softly and carry a big stick."[1]

—Theodore Roosevelt

Radical Islamic groups are not simply isolated sub-State religious terror cults like Japan's Aum Shinrikyo. According to a thought provoking special report from *Newsweek* entitled, "Why Do They Hate Us," these terrorists "come out of a culture that reinforces their hostility, distrust and hatred of the West—and of America in particular."[2]

Similarly, these Islamic zealots are far different from mere criminals. Unlike criminals, they are not in it for monetary gain. They do not wish to circumvent the system, rather they desire to destroy the system. Their fantastic goal is to create an Islamic caliphate that controls the world. Still, al-Qa'eda and other radical Islamic groups will cite numerous grievances against the United States to justify their "defensive" use of terror including American support of puppet Arab governments, importation of oil, support

---

1. A popular phrase often used by Theodore Roosevelt in the context of American foreign policy. President Roosevelt attributed it to a West African proverb.
2. Fareed Zakaria, *The Politics of Rage: Why Do They Hate Us?*, NEWSWEEK, October 14, 2001.

149

for Israel, Westerners living in Arab lands, morally corrupt Western culture, and so on. These complaints are hollow. Like all enemies of freedom and pluralism, be it the German Nazis or the Stalinist Communists, the radical Islamic terrorists attack the West for what it is, not for what it has done.

In a nutshell, the anti-Americanism is motivated by religious enmity, and militant Islamic terrorist groups have no regard or respect for human life, let alone the human rights and fundamental freedoms of others. In this vein, the overall problem is not the acts of terror but the mindset of those behind the terror attacks.

In early 2015, General Martin Dempsey, the Chairman of the Joint Chiefs of Staff, testified before Congress about long-term and short-term solutions to defeat ISIS. General Dempsey said that the only long-term solution to defeat ISIS was to defeat its "ideology." "We can harden the region [the Middle East] against it [ISIS] militarily, but the ideology has to be defeated."[3]

Of course, Dempsey knew full well that it was a religious belief that motivated ISIS and radical Islam, not an "ideology," but he was constrained in his vocabulary by the superciliousness of the Obama Administration with its refusal to use the term religion or radical Islam in the same breath with ISIS. But Dempsey had it right. The long-term solution means shutting down the "Hitler Youth Camps" of radical Islam.

Dempsey also suggested that the long-term solution to stop ISIS should be spearheaded by fellow Muslims in the region, they should do the heavy lifting to defeat the influence of the religion of radical Islam. This is a wonderful suggestion, often voiced, but there is slim evidence that anything of significance is being done to accomplish this lofty goal, either by Muslims in the Middle East or anywhere else.

Dempsey's view regarding the short-term solution, to harden the area in the Middle East is also militarily correct, but impossible to accomplish under the current American strategy of swatting a few bees around the beehive. Dempsey knew that the Obama strat-

3. Senate Foreign Relations Committee Meeting, Martin Dempsey, Joint Chiefs of Staff Chairman, March 11, 2015.

egy of limited force through a weak-kneed coalition would not bear
fruit.

In turn, the Arab League leaders will not take the lead to defeat
ISIS. Knowing full well that the U.S. will not provide the protective
umbrella or leadership they have seen in the past, Arab countries
are content to also engage in form over substance. Indeed, the idea
that Middle Eastern countries will unite and donate the capabilities to win on a voluntary basis has been tried before and it always
fails.

So what to do? There are workable long-term and short-term
strategies that even Helen Keller could figure out. Everything begins, however, with understanding the true nature of our adversaries.

Know Your Enemy

Encapsulated in every strategy to blunt radical Islamic terrorism is
the need to directly address the question of what causes these people
to engage in the murder of innocent civilians? At its core the movement is fueled by a red hot religious zeal that can only be quenched
when all infidels who stand in opposition are converted, conquered,
or killed. This is abundantly clear, but seldom recognized.

Shielded by an American society that is hypersensitive to the
cult of political correctness, Islamists have been able to operate and
spread their propaganda in the United States and the West with little
difficulty. When confronted about the goals of radical Islam, Muslim adherents are very adept at using our own freedom of speech
and freedom of religion against us. They know that few Americans
seem willing to point out the obvious—these people murder in the
name of a particular religious belief which is contained in Islamic
dogma.

In addition, since the start of the Obama Administration, the
proclamation from on high—in word and deed—has been that radical Islam is not a top priority threat to the nation. Wishing that this
assessment by their government was valid, many Americans are all
too willing to hit the snooze button on the alarm clock. With the rise
of ISIS, however, the nation has begun to heed the wake-up call.
The War on Terror is not over. In fact, it is intensifying.

Surprisingly, and contrary to the fears of America's leadership, many Muslims around the world are very satisfied to recognize the label of radical Islam as valid. They know the enemy. It is in this way that they are able to separate their Islam from the Islamic beliefs that energize the terrorists. Logically, instead of shunning the reality of radical Islam, the United States should name names as a way to separate radical Islam from the Islam most Muslims practice. As noted, President Obama persisted throughout with the notion that because radical Islamic actions and beliefs do not align with peaceful Islamic actions and beliefs, that the extremists cannot possibly be acting pursuant to Islam.

Currently, the two greatest threats in terms of radical Islam are Iran and ISIS. They blatantly tell us they want to kill us. I believe them. The French apparently do too and have shifted from similar polices of denial to actually identifying radical Islam as the culprit.

On January 7, 2015, the terror attacks by radical Muslim jihadists in Paris at the offices of *Charlie Hebdo* and the Jewish market captured the world's attention and brought a new focus to France's approach to radical Islam. The situation in France has now reached critical mass, not because the Muslim population in France is six million people, fast approaching the number of French practicing Catholics,[4] but because many of these Muslims support jihad.

Apart from the fact that many Europeans are intimidated by the large numbers of Muslims living amongst them who refuse to adopt Western cultural and law, is the fact that tens of thousands of young European Muslims have willingly joined the ranks of radical Islam, with many thousands leaving Europe to join the caliphate in Syria and Iraq.

France and the rest of Europe is now asking "Why?" According to one commentator: "It is time for us to break, once and for all, with the Leninist reasoning that has been served up for so long by the useful idiots of a radical Islam immersed in the sociology of

4.   John D. Snethen, *The Crescent and the Union: Islam Returns to Western Europe*, INDIANA JOURNAL OF GLOBAL LEGAL STUDIES, Volume 8: Issue 1, Article 14, (2000).

poverty and frustration."[5] In other words, it is not poverty or "alienation" that is the problem—it is religion.

French Prime Minister Manual Valls said: *"Oui, la France est en guerre contre le terrorisme, le djihadisme et l'islamisme radical"* (Yes, France is in a war against terrorism, jihadism, and radical Islamism).[6]

> We are at war — not a war against a religion, not a war against a civilization, but to defend our values, which are universal .... It's a war against terrorism and radical Islamism .... The French people need to stand up for freedom of speech and faith—which in France means keeping religion separate from government .... Everyone must take responsibility—politicians and citizens alike. We cannot let pass a single one of these messages, or a single one of these acts. Our indignation must be clear, total and last longer than three days. It must be permanent. We need standards, values and authority. There must be a firm message about the values of the republic and secularism.[7]

The French now implore their Muslims in France to take a stand against radical Islam. This is the correct approach. As stated twice before in this book, the bottom line issue is not whether Islam is in fact inherently violent; rather, what do the billion plus Muslims around the world believe and how many of these are willing to engage in jihad?

---

5. Bernard-Henri Levy, *A France United Against Radical Islam*, WALL STREET JOURNAL, January 8, 2015, at A1.

6. Tommy Christopher, *FOX NEWS and NPR Wonder Why Obama Won't Say 'Radical Islam' After He Said 'Radical Islam,'* THE DAILY BANTER, January 13, 2015, at A1, http://thedailybanter.com/2015/01/fox-news-npr-wonder-obama-administration-refuses-say-radical-islam/.

7. *Delicate Balance: Fighting Extremist Islamists While Guarding Against Anti-Muslim Backlash*, HOMELAND SECURITY NEWS WIRE, January 15, 2015, http://www.homelandsecuritynewswire.com/dr20150115-delicate-balance-fighting-extremist-islamists-while-guarding-against-antimuslim-backlash.

Assessing the Power of Radical Islam

Again, the vision of radical Islam is a never-ending jihad which mimics the seventh century jihad of Muhammad—the spread of Islam by force of arms. Unless and until they are shut down, the War on Terror cannot be won. Secretary of Defense Donald Rumsfeld made this point early on in an October 2003 memorandum he sent to General Richard Myers, Chairman of the Joint Chiefs of Staff, entitled: *Global War on Terrorism*. In the memorandum, Rumsfeld asked:

> Are we capturing, killing or deterring and dissuading more terrorists [jihadists] everyday than the madrassas [sic] and the radical clerics are recruiting, training, and deploying against us?[8]

Are we winning? In a February 2015 front page story in *USA Today*, President Obama proclaimed that "ISIL [sic] is going to lose."[9] Nice Obama rhetoric, but with America content to sit on the sidelines, it is hard to see how ISIS is going to lose.[10] As of now, ISIS is winning.[11] They have zero fear of America.

In turn, with the disastrous Iran nuclear deal concluded by the Obama Administration and approved by the United Nations Security Council, Iran will have nuclear weapons, probably before 2025.[12] Just a week after the deal was signed, Ayatullah Ali Khamenei, Iran's Supreme Leader, proclaimed: "Our policy toward the arrogant U.S. government won't change at all."[13] A nuclear armed Iran will flex their totalitarian muscles as never before, threaten

8. Donald Rumsfeld, *Rumsfeld's War-On-Terror Memo*, USA TODAY, May 20, 2005, at A1, http://usatoday30.usatoday.com/news/washington/executive/rumsfeld-memo.htm.
9. Gregory Korte, *Obama: 'ISIL is Going to Lose,'* USA TODAY, February 12, 2015, at A1.
10. *See* Michael Crowley, *Coalition of the Wary*, TIME, September 29, at 25 (describing the weak American led coalition to stop ISIS).
11. See Bill Powell, *Is ISIS Winning?*, NEWSWEEK, June 12, 2015, at 12.
12. Joe Lauria, *U.N. Endorses Nuclear Deal with Iran*, WALL STREET JOURNAL, July 21, 2015, at A6.
13. Ayatullah Ali Khamenei, TIME, August 2, 2015, at 5.

the West as "equals," spark nuclear proliferation in the region, and perhaps serve as the key element in their global apocalyptic dream of bringing in the end times of Allah. As of now, Iran is winning. They have zero fear of America.

There Is No Substitute for Military Victory

When I go to bed at night, I don't worry about the French or the British attacking the United States with a WMD. I do worry about Iran and ISIS. Why? Because the former are democracies and the later are not. The foreign policy of Teddy Roosevelt to "speak softly and carry a big stick" is in keeping with conservative thinking on how to deal with other nations and peoples. To our friends we can speak softly by means of dialogue about disagreements, but to our enemies we have nothing to say. To our enemies we either use or threaten to use the big stick of military force.

Thus, whether we are going to use it in fact or use it to "rattle the saber" in deterrence, America needs a large and well trained military. Pacifists insist on speaking softly and shunning violence. They always prefer to walk softly with our enemies. Consequently, pacifists are quick to cut the armed forces of America at the drop of the hat, but never ever do they advocate for cutting food stamps, welfare, or other entitlements. Not only will they not fight when necessary, they are determined to hand us a McDonald's plastic butter knife to wave at our adversaries.[14]

Those who imagine that negotiations can solve things or prove effective in dealing with radical Islam might ask a jihadist: "What do you want?" "What can we in the West do to meet your demands so that you and I can live in peace and harmony?" The answer by the Islamist would be very direct: "I want to kill you."

Given the negotiating position of the jihadist, our range of counter-proposals are quite limited. Having visited GITMO myself as part of a U.S. Southern Command sponsored fact-finding team,

14. Baker Spring, *Disarm Now, Ask Questions Later: Obama's Nuclear Weapons Policy*, HERITAGE FOUNDATION 1 (July 12, 2013), http://www.heritage.org/research/reports/2013/07/disarm-now-ask-questions-later-obamas-nuclear-weapons-policy (Obama's desire to reduce America's nuclear program along with conventional military forces).

I have seen the jihadist up close and personal and there is no doubt that they are murderous religious fanatics. In the short-term, we either have to kill them or detain them.

Given that we must fight, no war can be won by playing defense. The side that takes the battle to their enemy will win. In strategy, defense is only employed to prepare the military for subsequent offensive action. America must take the offensive in a way that is far different than the largely cosmetic Obama approach to warfare. We must crush them. We must kill them and stack them like cord wood for a cold winter's night. Bush understood the value of over-whelming military force and he used it in 2001 to close down the al-Qa'eda camps in Afghanistan and drive the Taliban from power. Bush also absolutely crushed the largest military in the Middle East in the 2003 War with Iraq.

The only analysis that needs serious thought is: (1) whether or not the military action is legal; and (2) is it in our best national in-terest. Is it legal and is it smart?

The one and only time that President Obama unleashed our military was in the context of his massive air campaign against the dictatorship of Libya's Muammar Gaddafi in 2011. The President spearheaded a NATO effort (for all practical purposes the United States supplied 90 percent of the effort) to destroy Gaddafi with the naïve idea that a democratic government would take root. Of course, Gaddafi was driven out of power, but the results were a disaster for the United States, the region, and the world.[15] It was not a smart use of our military by any stretch of the imagination.

Colonel Gaddafi was indeed a "bad" guy, but practically every Muslim nation in the Middle East is ruled by a dictator. The bottom line is that Gaddafi posed no threat to the United States or any of his neighbors. On the contrary, Gaddafi had locked up in his jails all the radical Islamists in Libya and was making strides towards more openness in his rule (in 2003 he admitted to the State-sponsored terror attack over Lockerbie, Scotland and paid the families of the victims millions of dollars in compensation). Now, because of Pres-

---

15. Press Release, The White House, Remarks by the President in Address to the Nation on Libya (March 28, 2011).

ident Obama's counterproductive decision, all the radical jihadists are out of jail, heavily armed, and waging jihad up and down North Africa. Libya is a failed State and America has been driven out. By any measurement Obama made the situation worse, not better.

Now we have the dual problem of ISIS and Iran. First, the legal side of the equation. ISIS and Iran have threatened the United States with destruction and murdered U.S. citizens giving us the legal right under international and domestic law to make war on them. Second, is it in the best interest of our national security to destroy ISIS and to stop Iran from acquiring nuclear weapons? In both cases, even President Obama agreed that the answer is yes. Next, having made these determinations, real world short-term action must be taken. We either apply overwhelming violence or threaten to apply overwhelming violence.

Since ISIS and Iran are above the ground and easy targets, they are prime candidates for large scale military action. We lock and load and execute the mission with devastating military force delivered under the parameters of the law of war. Yes, it is just that simple.

Regarding ISIS. If the United States is serious about stopping ISIS, it is not enough to find the needle in the haystack with limited air strikes or drone attacks. The entire haystack must be burned to the ground. Once we obliterate the caliphate from the face of the earth, we leave and return to our own shores. To be sure there are those who will complain that killing them will do no good as they will simply reemerge someplace else. The answer to that issue is also simple. If and when that event occurs and if it is in our national interest to do so, we will return and crush that reincarnation as well, then leave again.

There is no substitute for military victory. This is not the millennium.[16] War, like crime, is the permanent condition of mankind. Under the provisions of the law of war, we must kill their leaders and fighters until they are dead and are dead gone.

---

16. Katherine Stark Tapping & Catherine Braden Yeammans, THE LEGACY OF THE DOCTRINAL TEACHINGS OF ROBERT B. THIEME, JR. 53–55 (2014) (discussing the Christian belief in a future Millennium period on the earth where Jesus Christ will rule a world at peace for 1,000 years from Jerusalem).

One thing is certain, such a move would obviously have a tremendous short-term benefit and it would provide great traction toward the long-term goal of blunting the religion of radical Islam. The once energized jihadists around the world would now fall silent, concluding that Allah was obviously not on the side of ISIS's caliphate and crawl back into their rat holes where they belong.

Regarding Iran. We either bomb them or they get the bomb. Yes, it is just that simple. After advising other Western and friendly allies in the region, the President of the United States sends the Ayatollahs an envelope which contains a shiny 45 caliber bullet and a note. The note reads: "You have 30 days to shut down your entire nuclear program." If they refuse, then the military option is executed. Recognizing the matter of unintended consequences, military force may include progressive levels of low-level action to include a sea blockade of Iran or limited bombing sorties of their energy production facilities.[17] Whatever it takes.

If You Break it You Own It

So what does it mean if we do use overwhelming military force against ISIS and Iran? Do we have any further requirement other than to destroy them and sweep them into the dustbin of history? During the run up to the 2003 War in Iraq, then Secretary of State Colin Powell was famously quoted as saying "If you break it, you own it," referring to the notion that America would have an obligation to assist in rebuilding the infrastructure of Iraq once we had destroyed Saddam Hussein's military in battle. This view is incorrect and not in keeping with conservative thinking. The correct observation about a defeated enemy nation would be: "If you break it, it is broken." The deterrence message will resonate and reverberate to both that nation and to surrounding totalitarian regimes. Our enemies will fear us and our friends will respect us.

America has absolutely no obligation to help rebuild any part of a defeated nation or people. In fact, as we have seen far too often

---

17. *See* Tom Vanden Brook, *Officials: Iran Attack Could Set Back Bomb Effort 2 Years*, USA TODAY, August 24, 2015, at A3 (discussing various military options for shutting down Iran's nuclear program).

in the Middle East, this is a fool's errand. Obviously, as long as American troops are willing to stay on the ground, they can keep the lid on, but when they leave the anti-democratic forces of Sharia Law will return with radical Islam following close behind, as was the case in Iraq and Afghanistan. Their narrative is: "We drove the United States out by the will of Allah," and thousands will flock to the banner of radical Islam. It is far better to advance our narrative: "The United States obliterated you and we will return if you attack us again."

But Somebody Might Get Hurt

Before departing the subject of the use of violence it is important to address the issue of those who reject the use of violence under any circumstances. Pacifists will chant that spurious misconception that "violence never solves anything." Really? Of course, violence solves things. What stopped Adolph Hitler was violence, and a lot of it. While violence should be used as a last resort the lawful use of violence is an inherent right and often a necessity.[18]

The voices in the War on Terror who call for peace at any price say nothing new. Advocating peace, but having no idea of what

---

18. *See* U.N. CHARTER art. 51. The analytical framework for the use of force is found in Article 51 of the U.N. Charter, which codifies the "inherent right of self-defense." The inherent right of self-defense refers to the right of a country to unilaterally engage in acts of self-defense; regardless of what any other nation or organization, to include the United Nations, may or may not do. This is a well-known and ancient component of international law.

> Nothing in the present Charter shall impair the inherent right of individual or collective self-defense if an armed attack occurs against a Member of the United Nations, until the Security Council has taken measures to maintain international peace and security. Measures taken by Members in the exercise of the right of self-defense shall be immediately reported to the Security Council and shall not in any way affect the authority and responsibility of the Security Council under the present Charter to take at any time such action as it deems necessary in order to maintain or restore international peace and security.

Id.

the concept must necessarily entail—the willingness to fight for peace—anti-war activists always seek appeasement.

Some religious leaders emotionally disturbed by the fact that large numbers of soldiers are killed in war, irrationally conclude that all war in the modern era is immoral, regardless of the motivation. Railing against the 2003 War in Iraq one high profile pacifist by the name of Guy Munger concluded that "any discussion of whether Desert Storm was a just war seem[s] to border on the insane. Indeed, practical application of the theory may have ended with the crossbow." According to Munger, "modern war is always immoral."[19] Of course, the argument is totally fallacious for two reasons. First, long before the crossbow, battle casualties could easily mount into the hundreds of thousands. For example, during the Second Punic War (219–202 BC), the Carthaginian forces under Hannibal killed in combat over 60,000 Roman soldiers in a single day. And second, Munger fails to understand the real world consequences associated with a refusal to defend oneself. Pacifism does nothing except encourage the ruthlessness of the aggressor.

Obviously, man is always confronted with aggression; a world without conflict is not something that is in the here and now. The attitude of any free people is to be well prepared for war so that the nation may either rattle the saber or, if necessary, employ the saber against the forces of aggression. Unfortunately, the sincere but unrealistic belief that war can be curtailed by third-party dispute settlement processes or by massive disarming processes is never abandoned. After receiving the 2002 Nobel Peace Prize in Oslo, Norway, former President Jimmy Carter concluded his December 10, 2002, remarks by asserting that God gives mankind the capacity for choice and that war is always an evil, even when necessary, and "never a good."[20]

---

19. *See* Jeffrey F Addicott, Terrorism Law: Materials, Cases, Comments, 392–397 (7th ed. 2014).

20. Jimmy Carter, Former U.S. President, Nobel Lecture, Oslo, Norway (Dec. 10, 2002), http://nobelprize.org/nobel_prizes/peace/laureates//2002/carter-lecture.html (accepting the Nobel Peace Prize, former President Jimmy Carter discussed his various roles in working toward global stability and the changes the world has seen since his term in office).

Sometimes, thankfully, liberals do see the light. In her 2006 book, *The Mighty and the Almighty*, even the liberal-minded Secretary of State Madeleine Albright opposed the voices of appeasement that protested the pending military campaign against the Taliban regime in Afghanistan following the attacks of 9/11. Not only did she disagree with the official 2001 call by the World Council of Churches to not strike back against al-Qa'eda, but she also questioned the soundness of prize winning author Alice Walker's bizarre admonishment that "the only punishment that works is love."[21]

Still, for the committed pacifist, there should be no relationship between religion and warfare. Their interpretation of religion prohibits all forms of violence whatsoever. Further, they steadfastly oppose people who invoke God to justify violence in self-defense. While one can certainly agree with the utopian idea that war, crime, poverty, and a whole host of evils should not exist in the world, it is a fact that they do. When asked by his disciples what would be the signs that would signal His second coming to the world, Jesus Christ himself declared that wars would continue to be a part of the landscape until His return: "And you will be hearing of wars and rumors of wars; see that you are not frightened, for those things must take place, but that is not yet the end."[22]

To some, pacifism is a fundamental aspect of being a "good" Christian. Liberals think that they are somehow reflecting the attitude and concepts of Jesus Christ by trying to abolish war. This is absurd. To use the Bible to justify an uncompromising belief in pacifism requires one to distort, ignore, or otherwise explain away vast areas of scripture that speak approvingly of specific instances where lawful violence is justified and necessary to protect various values and objects in self-defense. Violence is not justified if used as a pretense for aggression but it is justified if used in self-defense.

A fair understanding of the Bible does not support the human viewpoint expressed by the anti-war activist. In AD 425, Augustine, the Bishop of Hippo, strongly affirmed the idea that the Bible

21. *See* Madeleine Albright, THE MIGHTY AND THE ALMIGHTY 150–151 (2006).
22. *Matthew* 24:6.

does not prohibit or condemn a Christian from engaging in combat on the battlefield in the sphere of self-defense. In a letter to a Roman Christian by the name of Boniface, Augustine told him to fight the invading tribes called the Vandals because "[w]ar is waged in order that peace may be obtained."[23] As stated in *Ecclesiastes* and echoed throughout the Bible, in the affairs of mankind there is clearly "[a] time for war, and a time for peace."[24] The hope is that when a Christian goes to war, he will be militarily prepared, per *Psalms* 144:1—"[God] teach my hands to war and my fingers to fight"[25] —and that the national leadership will heed *Proverbs* 20:18, by choosing to "make war by wise guidance."[26]

23. Letter from St. Augustine to Boniface (AD 418), *in* 1 NICENE AND POST-NICENE FATHERS OF THE CHRISTIAN CHURCH 553-554 (Philip Schaff, ed., 1983).
24. *Ecclesiastes* 3:3, 8b.
25. *Psalms* 144:1 ("Blessed be the Lord my strength, which teaches my hands to war, and my fingers to fight.").
26. *Proverbs* 20:18.

Chapter 12

In the Long Haul

"Ne Incautus Futuri (not heedless of the future)."[1]

—The Lee Family Motto

The key to winning the War on Terror in the long-term is to address the religious aspect of how radical Muslim leaders recruit and indoctrinate new followers. Interestingly, the suicide foot soldiers and their leaders defy simplistic political, sociological, or psychological profiling. They come from extremely diverse educational, economic, and social backgrounds; the only common red thread that binds them together is an unrelenting devotion to their radicalized Islamic belief system.

The motivations of these militant radical Islamic terror organizations are focused on the advancement of cult-like religious objectives rather than the more typical aspirations of traditional old-styled terrorist groups who are primarily concerned with the achievement of political or territorial goals. Related to the inherent dangerousness of radical Islamic terrorist groups, is the fact that States providing support to these people suffer from the scourge

---

1. Michael Korda, Clouds of Glory 1 (2014). This was the family motto of the Lees of Virginia. Robert E. Lee often used the phrase, "It is all in God's hands," not in a spirit of fatalism, but in one of unshakeable belief and confidence regarding God's Divine plan and will for his life and all mankind.

of totalitarianism and open hostility to America and the West. This is an important phenomenon not only because terror groups could probably not flourish into sophisticated networks without the overt support of a State, but also because they can use those States to launch catastrophic terror attacks. Iran is the perfect illustration.

Promote Democratic Freedoms

One long-term solution rests in the fact that democracies do not sponsor or support terrorism, dictatorships do.[2] There exists an abundance of empirical evidence that stable democracies do not engage in international terrorism, instigate war, engage in democide (genocide and mass murder), or abuse the human rights of their people. As Anthony Lake, a Clinton era special assistant to the president for national security affairs, related in an address at John Hopkins University: "Democracies tend not to wage war on each other and they tend not to support terrorism—in fact, they don't. They are more trustworthy in diplomacy and they do a better job of respecting the...human rights of their people."[3]

National Security Law expert and Director of the Center for National Security Law at the University of Virginia School of Law, Professor John Norton Moore, argues that totalitarian regimes are considerably more likely to resort to aggressive violence than democracies. Professor Moore terms this phenomenon the "radical regime" syndrome:

> A radical totalitarian regime ... seems to blend together a mixture of a failing centrally planned economy, severe limitations on economic freedom, a one-party political system, an absence of an independent judiciary, a police state with minimal human rights and political freedoms at home, a denial of the right to emigrate, heavy involvement of the military in political leadership, a large percentage of the

2. NATIONAL SECURITY LAW 61 (John Norton Moore & Robert F. Turner eds., 2d ed. 2005).
3. See John Norton Moore, SOLVING THE WAR PUZZLE, 102 (2004); Anthony Lake, Speech on "From Containment to Enlargement," John Hopkins University, Washington, D.C., September 21, 1993.

GNP devoted to the military sector, a high percentage of the population in the military, leaders strongly motivated by an ideology of true beliefs including willingness to use force, aggressively anti-Western and antidemocratic in behavior, and selective support for wars of national liberation, terrorism, and disinformation against Western or democratic interests.[4]

Understanding Moore's framework would lead to policies that would confront the totalitarian regime, not appease it.

Certainly, in the preamble to the U.N. Charter and in Article 1 of the Charter,[5] it is evident that the drafters also understood that nations who respect human rights and fundamental freedoms are less likely to engage in terrorism. This truth is axiomatic and democracies should be much more critical of totalitarian regimes to include countries that embrace Sharia Law.

Sadly, although the drafters of the UN Charter writing in San Francisco in 1945 understood the importance of democratic ideals, the United Nations has degenerated into a worthless organization. Today, and for a long time, any nation—dictator or democratic—is eligible for membership and totalitarian regimes are set on equal footing with freedom loving nations.[6] If the West was really serious about promoting peace and democracy, a new international organization would emerge with membership only offered to nations that actually adhered to the goals of peace, human rights, and freedom.

---

4. *Id.*

5. *See* U.N. Charter art. 1; U.N. Charter art. 2, para. 3; U.N. Charter art. 2, para. 4. The maintenance of international peace and security is, in fact, the very purpose of the United Nations. No nation may resort to the "threat or [the] use of force against the territorial integrity or political independence of any State" to settle any form of dispute. This, and the clear prohibition in Article 1 against any nation committing "acts of aggression or other breaches of the peace," creates a legal framework dedicated to curtailing unlawful aggression.

6. *Democracy's Decline: Crying for Freedom,* Economist (Jan. 14, 2010), http://www.economist.com/node/15270960 (According to the lobby group Freedom House, the number of electoral democracies in the world stands at 116 out of the 192 [there are now 193 members] nations in the United Nations).

Immigration & Sharia Nations

Another long-term solution rests in restricting those who seek entry into Western nations to live. In America, much has been written about the necessity to secure our national borders from the influx of illegal aliens, not only because of the threat of radical Islam, but simply in terms of common sense. When the history books are written about the United States of America's refusal to properly secure its borders, objective historians will surely ponder the stupidly of a nation that allowed millions and millions of foreign illegal aliens into their country, many with nothing to offer expect a strong desire to partake of the social welfare programs of the State. Here is the bottom line: a social welfare State with open borders spells the end of the nation. I am for legal immigration and against illegal immigration.

In tandem with the problem of illegal aliens entering America is the matter of legal immigrants coming to America.[7] Legal immigrants must demonstrate that they will provide a benefit to America. Why would any nation open its arms to foreigners that do not share, let alone appreciate, the values of that nation? Unfortunately, since the 1970s, America's immigration laws have been driven by the doctrine of multiculturalism, admitting large numbers of people that have no appreciation or respect for traditional American values. This problem is particularly disconcerting when it comes to Muslims that emigrate from Sharia Law based countries. It is from this pool that radical Islam will draw many of its converts.

Obviously, with what we know about Sharia, Muslims who wish to be considered for admission to the United States must forsake Sharia Law and demonstrate clear and convincing evidence that they will wholeheartedly adopt the core values of freedom and Anglo-Saxon law. They must be willing to integrate into the nation that they immigrate to. It is for them to change their lifestyle, not America.

America is not a cauldron of hate. Americans are neither racist nor xenophobic, they have accepted many immigrants from across

---

7. *See* John Garcia & Ruth Ellen Wasem, Congressional Research Service RL32572, Immigration: Terrorist Grounds for Exclusion and Removal of Aliens (January 12, 2010).

the globe (the reverse is not true in Sharia nations). America is a land of tolerance, but it is also a land of freedom. Under the rubric of freedom, Congress must legislate a new immigration policy that pays special scrutiny to anyone coming from a country that is based on Sharia Law, in whole or in part. Obviously, such people have no frame of reference for the sacred values of freedom codified in our Constitution. One and all, they are attracted to our prosperity, but the question of loyalty to our core American values must be carefully tested. Furthermore, we know that radical Islam fully embraces the jihad concept of encouraging fundamentalist Muslims to migrate to non-Muslim nations with the eventual goal of capturing the land for Allah through a demographic avalanche of greater and greater numbers, even if it takes 100 years or more. These types of Islamic immigrants have no desire to give up Sharia when they come to America. They do not come here to make themselves "America compliant," they are here to make America "Sharia compliant."

As previously noted, Sharia Law is 100 percent incompatible with the values sacred to the democratic State. Sharia Law has nothing but antipathy for the genius founders of the United States of America who established a nation on the bedrock of limited government and the protections set out in the Bill of Rights. As long as the leaders and the people—born here and legal immigrants—remain faithful to those concepts, prosperity and freedom will continue to flourish.

This is America. America is a homeland for Americans, not a homeland for Muslims that embrace Sharia Law above our Constitution.

Promote Americanism

In two short sentences in the Declaration of Independence, the framers laid out a fantastic manifesto that recognized the God-given right of free men to form a government that would protect the fundamental freedoms of its citizens. For the original Americans, these rights were rooted in Divine providence, which made them inalienable and morally justified *ab initio*. In bold strokes, the Declaration of Independence proclaimed:

We hold these truths to be self-evident, that all men are created equal, that they are endowed by their Creator with certain inalienable rights that among these are Life, Liberty,
and the pursuit of Happiness. That to secure these rights,
Governments are instituted among Men, deriving their just
powers from the consent of the governed.

With their freedom purchased through six long years of blood-
shed on the battlefield, the colonial Americans produced one of the
most phenomenal documents in the history of mankind—the Constitution of the United States of America. Despite Abraham Lincoln's
perversion of the concept of *consent* as stated in his Gettysburg
address (a government based on the consent of the people does not
allow for illegal violence to force that consent),[8] the Constitution
predicates the very existence of government on the consent of the
people, leaving the people free to operate under lawful self-determination. Again, this means limited government. Taken from our
own Preamble to the Constitution, the primary responsibilities of
the federal government are: (1) to *provide* for the common defense,
by maintaining a strong national military force; and (2) to *promote*
the general welfare, by encouraging the free market system of capitalism and private ownership of property while enforcing civil law
and criminal law to protect law abiding citizens (italics added).

If nothing else is clear, it is certain that our founding fathers
were students of human nature. The Constitution and its Bill of
Rights were designed to limit power in order to protect individual
rights. They knew two fundamental truths: (1) that power tends to
corrupt those people in power;[9] and (2) that the nation is only as
strong and vibrant as the moral fiber of its people.

8.   *See* John Avery Emison, Lᴉɴᴄᴏʟɴ Uʙᴇʀ Aʟʟᴇs (2009); Thomas J. Dilorenzo,
Tʜᴇ Rᴇᴀʟ Lᴉɴᴄᴏʟɴ (2003). The speech held that the Federal soldiers who died
at the battle of Gettysburg in 1863 sacrificed their lives for the cause of self-
determination in order that a "government of the people, by the people,
and for the people, should not perish from the earth." This is blatantly false.
Consent of the governed does not come at the point of a bayonet. The Confederate soldiers fought for the right of self-determination, not the Federals.
9.   British historian Lord John Dalberg-Acton wrote in the early 19th century: "All power tends to corrupt; absolute power corrupts absolutely."

Unfortunately, inherent in every democracy rest the seeds which will ultimately destroy it, for the real power rests not in the structure of the democratic government but in the character of the people that make up the nation. The South's greatest son, General Robert E. Lee, once observed that when virtue is absent from the people, the nation will collapse.[10] In other words, the freedoms and blessings associated with capitalism and free enterprise cannot function without virtue.

If Lee was correct, then it is necessary to ask ourselves what it means to have virtue. It is certainly a term that has limited impact in today's America, where the forces of political correctness run rampant across the land. Relative to the Americans of past generations that embraced self-reliance, hard work, family, and patriotism, America is a decaying society from top to bottom. The music, dress, language, manners, mores, and all forms of social intercourse reflect a culture in a frantic search for happiness with no sense of what it means to be an American. Postmodernism, multiculturalism, presentism and the abandonment of absolute concepts of privacy, property, family, and nationalism spell disaster for the country.

The "living, breathing Constitution" is the mantra of the progressive who seeks to distort the Constitution to fit the degeneracy of a clueless people victimized by political correctness. For such, the Constitution is the Devil's playground because, like abstract art, if it can mean anything, it means nothing.

In opposition to the voice of the progressive is the conservative who seeks to mold the people to the parameters set out in the Constitution. Thus, the conservative mind, like Supreme Court Justice Clarence Thomas, looks to the authors of the Constitution to see what *they* meant when *they* penned the words. For example, if the liberal contends that the death penalty constitutes "cruel and unusual punishment,"[11] and is therefore unconstitutional, the matter is settled by looking to the original intent of the founders. Indeed, as a Texan once quipped, the founders would unanimously respond

---

10. J. William Jones, Personal Reminiscences of General Robert E. Lee 223 (1875); H. W. Crocker III, Robert E. Lee on Leadership (1999).
11. U.S. Constitution, VIII Amendment.

to the matter of the legality of the death penalty by saying: "Get a rope!" Of course it is Constitutional.

In keeping with the fact that conservatism is profoundly simple, virtue is best defined as "doing a right thing in a right way." For instance, when the employer possesses virtue there is no need for workers to form unions because the boss will take better care of the wants and needs of his employees than any union ever could. In contrast, an employer without virtue will operate the company with selfish interests without regard to honesty and integrity. In turn, a worker with genuine virtue will work earnestly. Without virtue, a worker will produce little except slothfulness.

Where does virtue come from? Virtue cannot be legislated; it must be taught in the nuclear family home and reflected in the values of the society. America, which once prided itself on the "Protestant work ethic," increasingly rejects so-called "family values" related to marriage and the raising of children, and instead looks to a bloated central government to provide for its needs from the cradle to the grave.

In tracing the life expectancy of great democracies, it is interesting to note the words of historian Alexander Fraser Tytler (1748–1813), who wrote about the decline and fall of the Athenian Republic. Tytler concluded:

A democracy cannot exist as a permanent form of government. It can only exist until the voters discover that they can vote themselves money from the public treasury. From that moment on, the majority always votes for the candidates promising the most benefits from the public treasury with a result that a democracy always collapses over loose fiscal policy always followed by dictatorship.[12]

Considering that the United States of America is fast approaching its 250th anniversary, Mr. Tytler went on to develop a fascinating general trend in the rise and fall of the great nations. He wrote:

---

12. Alexander Fraser Tytler, THE DECLINE AND FALL OF THE ATHENIAN REPUBLIC (1776).

The average age of the world's greatest civilizations has been 200 years. These nations have progressed through the following sequence:
From bondage to spiritual faith;
From spiritual faith to courage;
From courage to liberty;
From liberty to abundance;
From abundance to selfishness;
From selfishness to complacency;
From complacency to apathy;
From apathy to dependency;
From dependency back to bondage.[13]

Where is America on Tytler's continuum? Even if many Americans apparently reject the values and norms of Americanism, there is still hope that there will be a rebirth of conservatism. Perhaps another great depression will wash away the dead weight, or perhaps a major military defeat will wake the people. In the interim, it makes no sense to allow immigrants into our nation that flatly reject our system of government and wish to replace it with a Sharia system of rule. Sharia Law is a repressive system that rejects Daniel Webster's America as "a state of society characterized by tolerance toward minorities, freedom of expression, and respect for the essential dignity and worth of the human individual with equal opportunity for each to develop freely to his fullest capacity in a cooperative community."[14]

Promote Christianity
The final long-term solution centers on the undeniable, positive influence of Biblical Christianity on mankind. Biblical Christianity is the most powerful tool available to defuse radical Islam. Apart from addressing the ultimate question—the eternal salvation of the human soul apart from human effort—its collateral temporal messages related to privacy protections, free enterprise, and freedom

13. *Id.*
14. Webster's Third New International Dictionary (1993).

of religion provide a blueprint solution for rebuffing the obscene propaganda of radical Islam.

America's founding fathers understood that following certain pillars of establishment as taught in the Bible would unleash untold prosperity and freedom. Hence, they folded these Bible-based concepts into our Constitution and the Bill of Rights. These same forces can blunt radical Islam, particularly when it comes to freedom of religious belief.

The Bible-centered Christian theologian R. B. Thieme, Jr., called these temporal establishment principles, designed by God to provide stability in the human race, the Laws of Divine Establishment.[15] They consist of four institutions set out in the Bible: (1) privacy rights of the individual to use his volition to think, worship, and speak as he wishes;[16] (2) the institution of marriage between one man and one woman;[17] (3) the institution of the nuclear family to raise children;[18] and (4) nationalism, where the national entity operates under free enterprise capitalism and provides for a strong police and military force for the common defense.[19]

Ignoring the Laws of Divine Establishment stifles human rights and freedom and leads to tyranny and the inevitable collapse of society. Under privacy provisions, freedom of religious belief is a critical ingredient of a great nation and caused many people to flee Europe for a new life of religious freedom in America. As Thomas Jefferson said: "The Constitutional freedom of religion is the most inalienable and sacred of all human rights."

Virginia's aristocracy understood the importance as well. In 1786 the *Virginia Statute for Religious Freedom* was passed by the General Assembly. It held:

> [N]o man shall be compelled to frequent or support any religious worship place or ministry whatsoever, nor shall be

---

15. *See* R. B. Thieme, Jr., Divine Establishment (1973).
16. *Genesis* 2:17.
17. *Genesis* 2:24.
18. *See Genesis* 4; *Colossians* 3:20; *Ephesians* 6:1; *Deuteronomy* 6:6-9; 7:9.
19. *See Genesis* 10:5, 32; *Deuteronomy* 32:8; *Acts* 17:26-28; 1 *Peter* 2:13-18; *Colossians* 1:16; 2 *Thessalonians* 3:7-14.

enforced, restrained, molested, or burdened in his body or goods, nor shall otherwise suffer on account of his religious opinions or belief; but that all men shall be free to profess, and by argument to maintain their opinions in matters of religion, and that the same shall in no wise diminish, enlarge or affect their civil capacities.[20]

Because radical Islam feeds on an intolerant religious viewpoint that begins with Sharia and ends with the death cult of jihad, Muslim nations around the world can strike an immediate blow to the radical jihadists by enacting religious freedom reforms that abolish Islamic "blasphemy laws," common from Saudi Arabia to Pakistan. Under Sharia, blasphemy laws make it a criminal offense to say or do anything that is "insulting" to Islam. Punishments for blasphemy range from prison, floggings, and even death. For instance, only two days after the massacre in Paris by radical Muslims upset over the insult to Muhammad, the U.S. ally Saudi Arabia took a Muslim blogger convicted of "insulting Islam" from his prison cell to the front of the main mosque in the city of Jeddah and flogged him with a whip 50 times. Raif Badwai was sentenced to ten years in prison and flogging 50 times every week for 20 weeks.[21]

Although abolishing blasphemy laws will not happen in our lifetimes, such a move by the Arab world would directly assist in draining the swamps that breed radical Islam. For now, Muslim fundamentalism is too strong to see such reform.

Second, because radical Islam is primarily concerned with fulfilling Allah's will of conquering the world through jihad, the alternative view of God's will contained in Christianity is a fantastic countermeasure for non-violence. While it is true that as a works-religion Islam can certainly counter the voices of radical Islam that assert immediate entrance to paradise by self-sacrifice in jihad, it is Christianity alone that provides a message devoid of any form of human merit as the mechanics for evangelism and salvation.

20. *Virginia Statute for Establishing Religious Freedom* (1786).
21. *Laws Against Blasphemy Empower Muslim Extremists*, USA TODAY, January 15, 2015, at A7.

The Christian doctrine of grace, unique among all other religions, is the ultimate rebuke to radical Islam. Christianity is dogmatic in its orthodoxy, but absolutely rejects coercion in spreading its message of salvation. Christianity fully recognizes human freedom in the exercise of individual volition. Radical Islam does not.

Of all the major religions, Christianity has the largest number of followers and is the most widespread. Christians claim a direct extension from the Old Testament (*Genesis* 15:6 *cf Romans* 4:1-25),[22] and the Christian Bible incorporates with its New Testament all of the books of the *Tanakh* (the Old Testament), but under the concepts of abrogation and fulfillment. Therefore, the salvation message is the same in the Old Testament as in the New Testament—salvation by faith—but all the Old Testament rituals and mandates for the nation of Israel are no longer in effect for the Church Age.

The testimony of the person and work of Jesus of Nazareth, the Christ (*Christos* is the Greek word for the Hebrew word *Messiah*, *see Daniel* 9:25), is recorded in the New Testament through a series of letters written by either eyewitnesses of Christ or those directly associated with the eyewitnesses, from circa AD 40 (the earliest estimate for the book of *Matthew*) to circa 96 (the latest estimate for the book of *John*).[23] Although there are three major divisions—Roman Catholicism, Eastern Orthodoxy, and Protestantism—Christianity is a system of belief that begins and ends with the person of Jesus of Nazareth.

Biblical Christianity holds that Jesus is the promised Messiah written extensively about in the Old Testament—the Christ, the God/man[24]—who, while suspended on a Roman cross (circa AD 30), willingly bore God's righteous judgment for all human sins

---

22. *See* Huston Smith, THE WORLD'S RELIGIONS 221 (1991). The doctrine of the Trinity holds that "while God is fully one, God is also three. The latter half of this claim leads Jews and Muslins to wonder if Christians are truly monotheists, but Christians are confident that they are."

23. Ian Wilson, JESUS: THE EVIDENCE 11-23, 38-39 (1996). Wilson sets out dates for papyrus fragments from Matthew, John, and other New Testament texts that all date from the first century.

24. Lewis Sperry Chafer, 2 SYSTEMATIC THEOLOGY 386-387 (1947). The Chalcedonian declaration about Christ has been the standard of orthodox thinking about the nature of Jesus Christ for almost 1,500 years. It reads in part:

(*see Isaiah* 53; *Psalm* 22). During a three hour period in time, from 12:00 noon to 3:00 pm, God the Father imputed to the humanity of Jesus Christ[25] every sin that every human ever did and judged them all (*Matthew* 27:45). After three days in a tomb, Jesus Christ was raised from the dead in a resurrection body, seen by numerous witnesses, and 50 days later He ascended to heaven where He was accepted by God (1 *Corinthians* 15:12-20).

Although the Bible reveals that the attributes of God consist of love, sovereignty, omnipresence, omnipotence, omniscience, immutability, veracity, perfect happiness, and eternal life, God is also holy. God's holiness consists of two parts—absolute justice and absolute righteousness. Accordingly, because of His holiness, God cannot allow imperfect man—a sinner—to have eternal relationship with Him. If perfect God allowed imperfect man to have eternal relationship, God would have to compromise the other attributes of His perfect character. And this He cannot do.

The cosmic math problem is this:

Imperfect Man (-P) + Absolute Perfect God (+P) = Imperfection (–P).

God cannot allow man who is imperfect to have fellowship with

---

We, then, following the holy Fathers, all with one consent, teach men to confess one and the same Son, our Lord Jesus Christ, the same perfect Godhead and also perfect Manhood; truly God and truly man, of a reasonable [rational] soul and body; consubstantial [co-essential] with the Father according to the Godhead, and consubstantial with us according to the Manhood; in all things like unto us, without sin; begotten before all ages of the Father according to the Godhead, and in these latter days. For us and for our salvation, born of the Virgin Mary.

Id.

25. *See, e.g., 1 John* 2:2 ("And He Himself is the propitiation for our sins [believers]; and not for ours only, but also [for those of] the whole world."); *John* 1:29 ("Behold the Lamb of God, which taketh away the sins of the world."); *Matthew* 1:21 ("And she shall bring forth a son, and thou shalt call his name JESUS: for he shall save his people from their sins."); *Luke* 2:11 ("For unto you is born this day in the city of David a Saviour, which is Christ the Lord.").

perfection, Himself. Thus, if you wish to live with God you must be as good as God. Your human righteousness must be equivalent to His perfect righteousness.

Given the perfect nature of God, His holiness is a separation wall that no human can pass over, under, through, or around. Clearly, the righteousness of human morality cannot provide a relationship with God as works-religion asserts. As an analogy, suppose you and I decide that we are going to swim from Miami Beach, Florida, to the coast of France. No matter how good of a swimmer you may be, or I may be, or any person may be, no human will ever make it. The distance is too great.

So it is with achieving a relationship with perfect God. Even if a person could have every good deed that every human ever did credited to his "bank account" for presentation to God, it would still be deficient (*Revelation* 20:11–15).

In addition to the problem of our relative righteousness is the issue of our human sin. This is an impossible barrier as well. Not only are all humans born with a sin nature inherited from Adam, all humans use their volition to commit verbal sins, overt sins, and mental attitude sins. The Bible reveals that the penalty for sin is *spiritual* death—separation from God (*see Romans* 6:23). Even one sin is all it takes to be spiritually dead, but humans commit many sins over the course of a lifetime. Adam and Eve died spiritually at the moment of their single sin (disobeying God), but lived physically for a number of years in mortal bodies (*Genesis* 3).

God's perfect justice cannot waive sin, overlook sin, or have anything to do with sin except to condemn it. That is the bad news.

The good news is that God's attribute of love found a way to solve the unsolvable problems of man's sin and man's relative righteousness. He did this by a plan He developed in eternity past whereby the Second person of the Godhead would become a true man in hypostatic union and to pay the penalty of sin—spiritual death. Only Jesus Christ was qualified to take our place because He was the only human ever born on this planet that was born without a sin nature and never sinned.

Those humans that respond to this work of God on their behalf are instantaneously saved and God imputes His own perfection, the very righteousness of God,[26] to every believer in Christ. Also, at the second of belief in Christ, God gives the new believer His own eternal life. With sin removed and God's (+P) righteousness imputed to Man the cosmic math problem is solved.

> For God so loved the world [God's love motivated Him to address the problem of mankind in a state of sin] that He gave His only begotten [uniquely born] Son, that whosoever believes in Him shall not perish [eternal separation from God] but have eternal life [with God]. *John* 3:36

> He who knew no sin [the perfect humanity of Jesus Christ] was made sin for us that we might have the righteousness of God in Him [Christ]. 2 *Corinthians* 5:21.

> He [Jesus] bore our sins in His own body on the cross, so that we, being dead to sin, might have a new life in righteousness. 1 *Peter* 2:24

Thus, the penalty of human sin was dealt with by means of Christ taking our place and bearing the judgment for all human sin during the last three hours on the cross. The technical theological term is *unlimited atonement*.[27] The substitutionary spiritual

---

26. *See, e.g., Romans* 4:5 ("For the one who does not work, but believes in Him who justifies the ungodly, his faith is reckoned as righteousness."); 2 *Corinthians* 5:21 ("He [God the Father] made Him [Jesus Christ] who knew no sin to be sin on our behalf, that we might become the righteousness of God in Him"); *Galatians* 2:16 ("Nevertheless knowing that a man is not justified by the works of the Law but through faith in Jesus Christ, even we have believed in Christ Jesus, that we may be justified by faith in Christ, and not by the works of the Law; since by the works of the Law shall no flesh be justified."); *Romans* 3:24 ("Being justified as a gift by His grace through the redemption which is in Christ Jesus."); *Romans* 4:5 ("But to the one who does not work, [for salvation] but believes in Him who justifies the ungodly, his faith is reckoned [credited] as righteousness.").
27. The concept of unlimited atonement is found in a number of passag-

death of Christ means that all the sins of each member of the human race—past, present, and future—were imputed by God the Father and judged in Christ. He took our place. He was our substitute.

Again, this historical[28] fact does not automatically save any member of the human race, but it does make every member of the human race a candidate for salvation, because sin is taken off the table. To take advantage of the work of Christ on our behalf requires a simple act of non-meritorious faith (meaning no human works) in Christ. At that second in time God provides instantaneous and irrevocable salvation to any member of the human race who believes in Christ as his Savior, regardless of personal merit or moral worthiness of that person in the past or future—you cannot lose your salvation.[29] You are in the family of God.

Since entrance into an eternal relationship with God in time and eternity requires only a single speck of non-meritorious faith alone in Christ alone, this central doctrine of salvation is called the "gospel" or good news (*John* 3:16). In the planning, performance, and saving, it is totally the work of God, not man. Indeed, even the

---

es to include *2 Corinthians* 5:14-15, 19; *1 Timothy* 2:6: 4:10; *Titus* 2:11; *Hebrews* 2:9; *2 Peter* 2:1; *1 John* 2:2. For an excellent discussion of the work of Christ on the cross, *see* R. B. Thieme, Jr., THE BARRIER 21 (2003):

> When Christ hung on the cross, God imputed all the sins of the entire human race to Him and judged them. He was sinless Himself and, therefore, uniquely qualified to be our substitute. He bore in His own body on the cross every sin we have committed or ever will commit—past, present, and future (*1 Tim.* 4:10; *1 Pet.* 2:24). Our sins were charged to Christ, not to us. But until we accept His sacrifice by faith alone in Christ alone (*Eph.* 2:8-9), we retain our own relative righteousness.

Id.
28. *See* Josh McDowell, EVIDENCE THAT DEMANDS A VERDICT 83–89 (1972) (chronicles the historicity of Jesus from a variety of extra-biblical sources).
29. *See, e.g., Romans* 8:38-39 ("For I am persuaded, that neither death, nor life, nor angels, nor principalities, nor powers, nor things present, nor things to come, nor height, nor depth, nor any other creature, shall be able to separate us from the love of God, which is in Christ Jesus our Lord."). *See also* R.B. Thieme, Jr., THE PRODIGAL SON 6–7, 31–32 (1974) (setting out a detailed analysis of the Doctrine of Eternal Security).

"faith" that is exhaled by the hearer of the gospel is not sufficient to activate salvation, so that no Christian can boast that their degree of faith was greater than another's.

For instance, assume that A outputs 99 percent faith in Christ, B outputs 20 percent faith in Christ, and C outputs 0.00001 percent faith in Christ. Which one is saved? The answer = none of them. Even if a person had all the faith that every human that ever lived imputed to his faith "output" it would not be good enough. The grace of God takes the output of faith regardless of the amount (which could be the size of a mustard seed,[30] or in modern terms the size of an electron going around an atom) and He makes it efficacious for salvation.[31]

> For by grace are you saved through faith, and that [the entire grace system of salvation] not of yourselves, it is the gift of God, not of works, lest any man should boast. *Ephesians* 2:8-9.

This is grace. No one earns it or deserves it. While Christians should be upstanding citizens, moral, kind, forgiving, hard-working, etc., these things will not save. In salvation, God did all the work and God gets all the credit. Man can do nothing for salvation. Nothing.

Unlike other religions, whose founders could be entirely removed without destroying the noetic (intellectual) aspects of the religion, without the person and work of Jesus Christ, Christianity would cease to be. This is because the path set forth by Christianity to an eternal relationship with God (salvation) is not based on a system or formula of human works (morality, rituals, and so on) or philosophy, as all other types of works-religions dictate. Rather, it is based on the work of Jesus Christ while on the cross.

In the early years of Christianity, when the Roman persecution of Christians was heaviest, believers would use the symbol of the

---

30. *Matthew* 13:31-32.
31. *Titus* 3:5 ("He saved us, not on the basis of deeds which we have done in righteousness, but according to His mercy.").

fish as a recognition sign. As an encapsulated illustration to what Biblical Christians believe—then and now—the Greek letters that spell "fish" correspond to the words "Jesus Christ God's Son [the] Savior."

In summary, under Biblical Christianity one's eternal relationship with God is based absolutely and solely on a single act of personal belief in the redeeming work of the God/man Jesus Christ on the death-cross where He suffered "spiritual death" and became the substitute sacrifice for mankind's sin. Since Jesus Christ was the perfect God/man, He was qualified to bear the sins of the world and provide salvation to all who believe. This grace policy excludes all human merit as a means of salvation and thus stands in sharp contrast to all of the other major religions. Christianity is man accepting the work of God; all other religions are the notion that God will accept the work of man.

As previously discussed at Chapter 7, radical Islam amends the works-religion system of today's main-stream Islam and asserts that those who die in jihad do not go before the Judgment Seat of Allah for evaluation on their worthiness to enter heaven. Instead, these martyrs by-pass the judgment of Allah and automatically enter paradise to receive their eternal rewards which consist of numerous virgins. While some may find a "grace" element to this belief, it is not the grace concept of Biblical Christianity—the adherent has to kill himself, a substantial "work" which is done to gain the approbation of Allah.

Finally, the fact that vast numbers of people in the Church age have ignored the New Testament's clear mandates for tolerance and impersonal love towards all mankind does not reflect adversely on the Scriptures, but only on the nature of man. For example, the horrendous crimes perpetrated by the Spanish Inquisition 500 years ago in the name of Christ are not commanded in the New Testament. There is nothing to be "explained" away in the orthodoxy of Christianity, as there is in the orthodoxy of Islam.

Regardless of the fact that Christianity and Islam are diametrically opposed when it comes to the mechanics of salvation, Christianity is extremely valuable in the context of proclaiming the positive values of freedom of thought and deleting all actions that smack of force or violence to promote or spread the gospel. Further, Christians are commanded to examine and question their beliefs (1 *Thessalonians* 5:21) and to have a "live and let live" attitude towards all mankind (*Romans* 12:18). This is not in the purview of radical Islam.

Chapter 13

Conclusion

"The price of freedom is eternal vigilance."[1]
—George Washington

In a speech delivered in 1984, then United States ambassador to the United Nations, Jeanne J. Kirkpatrick, spoke of the coming "terrorist war [against the United States] ... as a total war which sees the whole society as an enemy, and all members of a society as appropriate objects for violent actions."[2] Her words came to pass on 9/11, they continue today with far greater urgency.

While attacks by radical Islam against American interests have yet to use a WMD (as of this writing), jihadists have demonstrated a viciousness and disregard for human life that ensures they will use such weapons at first opportunity. Essentially, time is not on the side of civilized nations as renegade regimes like Iran will sooner or later provide or use a WMD in the name of jihad. Unlike the situation in the Cold War, radical Islamic terrorists in the post 9/11 world do not even require a sophisticated delivery system. The suicide terrorist bomber is the delivery system. In addition, with the advent

---

1.   Kate Louise Robuts, NEW ENCYCLOPEDIA OF PRACTICAL QUOTATIONS 438 (1940).
2.   Jeanne J. Kirkpatrick, Speech at the Jonathan Institute's Conference on International Terrorism, Washington, D.C., (June 25, 1984).

of modern technology, the power to wage large-scale destruction has now passed from the arena of the nation-state into the realm of the individual.

The Americans of the "greatest generation" in the mid twentieth century faced an evil of their time in the form of Nazi Germany. In the handful of years before the outbreak of World War II, Adolph Hitler announced repeatedly what Nazi Germany intended to do in terms of violent acts against other peoples and nations. Many in the West denied it. Nazism was too horrible to conceive, therefore it must be false. Even in the face of raw Nazi aggression, they would not believe it. Instead of facing the reality of Nazism and meeting Hitler with a unified voice backed by lawful force, they cowered to him with the pedestrian polices of appeasement.

In their disorientation to reality, the preferred solution was to appease this evil movement that sought world domination in hopes that it would simply go away. And so in 1939, the Prime Minister of England, Neville Chamberlain, blissfully flew to Germany and "negotiated" a deal with Hitler that would ensure "peace in our time."

This strong signal of appeasement by the French and English was all the Nazis wanted. Hitler was encouraged to move forward, not backward. The ink on the agreement was barely dry before Hitler's military invaded Poland and World War II began.

Like the greatest generation in America, this generation has an evil of our time. The many-faced evil wears a single mask called radical Islam. Its ugly head has risen once again and is screaming "Death to America" in word and deed. Whether it is the radicalized Shia version (Iran) or the radicalized Sunni version, radical Islam is on a global march seeking nothing less than world domination. Denying the reality of jihadi murder might suit modern tastes, but it doesn't stand up to the overwhelming evidence of what is happening.

How are we meeting this challenge? In large part we are mimicking the Neville Chamberlains of history. We are in denial.

The forces of radical Islam arrayed against us are formidable. Their declared goal is to destroy us regardless if we recognize this as a reality or not. As one *National Review* author noted:

It's easy to see the appeal of imagining things to be other than they are. After all, the imaginary world of latent democracy and productive appeasement is so much kinder and gentler than the real world of jihad. But jihadists thrive on our imaginings – postponing their day of reckoning, and hastening ours.[3]

The Must-Do List

In the short-term we must use overwhelming military force against the major international players of radical Islam. This would be ISIS and Iran. Domestically, we must continue to employ the full weight of law enforcement against the jihadists who live amongst us. For the other radical Islamists that hide under the ground, like al-Qa'eda, we must continue to engage in asymmetric warfare using our special operations to full effect,[4] along with the power of enforceable monetary sanctions.[5]

In the long-term, the "Hitler Youth Camps" that preach jihadist propaganda must be confronted and closed down. Because radical Islam is religion driven, I argue that the influence of Christianity is a powerful force for good in this regard, but I also would support any program or process that stands up to radical Islam.

Obviously, we need to better educate ourselves about the jihadists and their religion. Bush and Obama consistently refused to irrevocably and sternly tell us that the conflict is with radical Islam—the "mother of all hate groups." This is beyond tragic and is a recipe for continued vacillation.

---

3. French, David, *Are ISIS Supporters Happy the President Won't Call Them "Muslim?"* NATIONAL REVIEW, February 25, 2015, http://www.national-review.com/corner/414393/are-isis-supporters-happy-president-wont-call-them-muslim-david-french.

4. *See* Bryan Bender, *DIA Chief Predicts Rise in "Asymmetric" Warfare,* DEFENSE DAILY, September 12, 1996. The term asymmetric warfare is of recent origin. It generally refers to unconventional conflicts against enemies that do not wear uniforms or follow the law of war.

5. For an excellent discussion of this see *Using a Civil Suit to Punish/Deter Sponsors of Terrorism: Connecting Arafat and the PLO to the Terror Attacks of the Second Intifada*, 4 ST. JOHN'S JOURNAL OF INTERNATIONAL AND COMPARATIVE LAW 71 (2014).

America must know the truth about our enemy. And yes, Americans can distinguish between the religion of Islam as practiced by the majority of Muslims and the religion of Islam as practiced by the jihadists. After 9/11, Americans did not light the torches and grab the pitchforks to attack Muslims, we understood the difference.

We must have true Statesmen to lead the nation. Leadership skills rooted in the panacea of dialogue and a "see where it takes us" approach in terms of national security are disastrous when confronting radical Islam and totalitarian fanatics. If the events of 9/11 have taught us anything, it is that the United States must lean forward in the saddle and operate from a position of strength under the law of war. The inability to set bright lines of clarity about radical Islam is not just a failure in definition, it is a failure in leadership and does tremendous damage to America's commitment to abide by the proper rule of law.[6]

With the end of the Obama Administration, America desperately needs a new Commander-in-Chief who possesses equal degrees of moral and strategic clarity.[7] Moral clarity means that he has the guts to lucidly articulate the evil of radical Islam so that the American people are fully informed. Strategic clarity means that he is willing to take direct action, divorced from political overtones, to institutionalize comprehensive policies that are fully rooted in the context of the lawful use of force.

As stressed in the voluminous *9/11 Commission Report* we must not suffer from "a lack of imagination,"[8] as we enter a more dangerous phase in the War on Terror.[9] The real possibility that a WMD

6. BLACK'S LAW DICTIONARY 1448 (9th ed. 2009). The rule of law is defined in Black's as a "substantive legal principle" and "[t]he doctrine that every person is subject to the ordinary law within the jurisdiction."
7. *See* Peter Baker, *Crises Cascade and Converge, Testing Obama*, N.Y. TIMES, July 22, 2014, at A1 (discussing how President Obama seems overwhelmed by the threats from Russia, Ukraine, Syria, Iraq, Afghanistan, Gaza, and the Middle East).
8. *See generally* 9/11 COMMISSION REPORT: FINAL REPORT OF THE NATIONAL COMMISSION ON TERRORIST ATTACKS UPON THE UNITED STATES 1–46 (2004).
9. Kevin Johnson, *9/11 Panel: Terrorism Fight is in 'New and Dangerous Phase'*, USA TODAY, July 22, 2014, at A1.

will be used against a large civilian population center is not an idle concern, it is a compelling call to action. All rational people can agree that the time to stop them is before they attack, not after. The United States of America needs a competent Commander in Chief who can lead in accordance with that premise and not airbrush the growing threat of radical Islam, before it is too late. By the grace of God.

About the Author

Jeffrey F. Addicott is a Professor of Law and the Director of the Center for Terrorism Law at St. Mary's University School of Law (www.stmarytx.edu/ctl), San Antonio, Texas, where he teaches a variety of courses to include National Security Law and Terrorism Law. An active duty Army officer in the Judge Advocate General's Corps for twenty years (he retired in 2000 at the rank of Lieutenant Colonel), Dr. Addicott spent a quarter of his career as the senior legal advisor to the United States Army's Special Forces. An internationally recognized authority in terrorism law, Professor Addicott not only lectures and participates in professional and academic organizations both in the United States and overseas, he is a frequent contributor to national and international media outlets.

Foreign presentations include numerous professional lectures at universities and government institutions in India, China, Sultanate of Oman, Colombia, Peru, Ukraine, Germany, France, Austria, Canada, Thailand, Japan, Honduras, Haiti, Egypt, Kuwait, Panama, Guatemala, Albania, Okinawa, Cuba, South Korea, England, Mexico, Sweden, Ireland, Scotland, Greece, Israel, Russia, and Uruguay. Presentations in the United States include over 800 appearances at universities, public and private State and Federal institutions, as well as more than 4,000 appearances on radio, print, and television broadcasts to include the Wall Street Journal, New York Times, Washington Post, Miami Herald, Dallas Star-Tribune, San Antonio Express-News, Los Angeles Times, Chicago Tribune, Washington Times, Washington Examiner, Reuters, Associated Press, Bloomberg, FOX NEWS Channel, MSNBC, CNN, ABC, PBS, NBC, CBS, NPR, BBC, Voice of Russia, and al-Jazeera.

Professor Addicott is a prolific author, publishing over sixty books, articles, and monographs on a variety of legal topics. Among his many contributions to the field, Professor Addicott pioneered the teaching of law of war and human rights courses to the militaries of numerous nascent democracies in Eastern Europe and Latin America. For these efforts he was awarded the Legion of Merit, named the "Army Judge Advocate of the Year" and honored as a co-recipient of the American Bar Association's Hodson Award.

Dr. Addicott served as the Associate Dean for Administration and Finance at St. Mary's University School of Law (2006-2007). He is also the 2007 recipient of St. Mary's University Alumni Association's "St. Mary's University School of Law Distinguished Faculty Award." Lieutenant Colonel Addicott (U.S. Army, ret.) served in senior legal positions in Germany, Korea, Panama, and throughout the United States. Professor Addicott holds a Doctor of Juridical Science (SJD) and Master of Laws (LLM) from the University of Virginia School of Law. He also received a Master of Laws (LLM) from the Judge Advocate General's School, a Juris Doctor (JD) from the University of Alabama School of Law and a bachelor of arts with "Honors in Government" (BA) from the University of Maryland.

Index

Terrorism Law: Materials, Cases, Comments, Seventh Edition

by Jeffrey F. Addicott, B.A., J.D., L.L.M., S.J.D.

An essential reference text on the War on Terror. As the first edition of Terrorism Law suggests, terrorism, like crime, can never be completely eradicated. Over the past few years, as previous editions were released, the United States has faced many changes and challenges pertaining to the War on Terror, and continues to do so today. Although it was realized at the time the war started that legal and policy challenges would exist, no one could have predicted exactly what events would occur. The seventh edition of Terrorism Law has been updated to include new developments in this war, including the Boston Marathon bombing, as well as some of our nation's and the world's biggest challenges while fighting it.

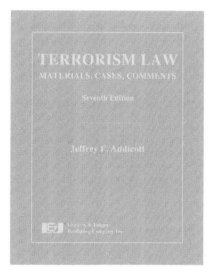

Topics include:
- What is terrorism?
- The Rule of Law: use of force
- Civil liberties and the War on Terror
- Addressing Terrorism since 9/11
- Interrogation techniques and what is torture
- Allegations of United States sanctioned torture
- Cyberterrorism
- Bioterrorism
- Civil litigation and the War on Terror

Product Code: 6028 • ISBN: 978-1-936360-17-8
Pages: 576 • Casebound • Size: 8.5″× 11″

Terrorism Litigation: Cases and Materials, Second Edition

by David Strachman

Terrorism law is an emerging field which has brought the "war on terrorism" into the courtroom. This new area of law has several unique features and has attracted widespread attention from academia, the media, the bar, and public interest groups.

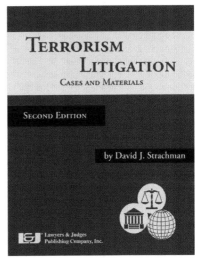

Terrorism Litigation, Second Edition, focuses on the law and practice of litigating claims of victims of international terrorism. Author David J. Strachman discusses the major landmark cases and explains applicable federal statutes. Strachman demonstrates the many differences between civil terrorism litigation, in which virtually all defendants are either rogue state sponsors of terrorism or designated terrorist organizations, and more common tort litigation which typically attempts to balance the conflicting claims of litigants.

This book is an essential reference for lawyers, law professors, political scientists and students. It also serves as a complete text for law school and undergraduate courses in terrorism law.

Topics Include:
- Historical attempts to bring terrorists to justice
- Alien Tort Claims Act of 1789
- Foreign Sovereign Immunities Act
- Antiterrorism and Effective Death Penalty Act of 1996
- Torture Victim Protection Act
- Terrorism Risk Insurance Act
- Acts of war
- Personal jurisdiction: states and non-states
- Punitive damages
- "Standard" terrorism damages
- Role of the U.S. government
- Payment of judgments

Product Code: 4462 • ISBN: 978-1-936360-10-9
Pages: 628 • Softbound • Size: 8.5″ × 11″